Fálki or Valur

Icelandic gyrfalcon, the national bird of Iceland.

Iceland Summer

ADVENTURES OF A BIRD PAINTER

by *George Miksch Sutton*

Illustrated by the author

NORMAN

UNIVERSITY OF OKLAHOMA PRESS

By George Miksch Sutton

Iceland Summer: Adventures of a Bird Painter (Norman, 1961)
Mexican Birds: First Impressions (Norman, 1951)
Birds in the Wilderness (New York, 1936)
Eskimo Year (New York, 1934)
The Exploration of Southampton Island, Hudson Bay
(Pittsburgh, 1932)
An Introduction to the Birds of Pennsylvania
(Harrisburg, 1928)

Illustrated by George Miksch Sutton

Fundamentals of Ornithology (by Josselyn Van Tyne and
Andrew J. Berger) (New York, 1959)
Georgia Birds (Norman, 1958)
World Book Encyclopedia (section on birds) (Chicago, 1941)
Birds of Western Pennsylvania (by W. E. C. Todd)
(Pittsburgh, 1940)
The Golden Plover and Other Birds (by A. A. Allen)
(Ithaca, 1939)
American Bird Biographies (by A. A. Allen) (Ithaca, 1934)
The Birds of Minnesota (in part) (by T. S. Roberts)
(Minneapolis, 1932)
The Burgess Seashore Book (in part) (by Thornton Burgess)
(Boston, 1929)
The Birds of Florida (by H. H. Bailey) (Baltimore, 1925)
A Guide to Bird Finding (by Olin Sewall Pettingill, Jr.)
(New York, 1951)

Library of Congress Catalog Card Number: 61–8998

*Here is a book for you—Father, Anne, Dorothy, Evie,
Harry, and Mark. I hope you like it.*

Foreword

It was forty years ago, in the middle of the night, that the idea of writing a book about Arctic birds took possession of me. I was alone at the wheel of the forty-five-foot motor yawl *Northern Messenger*, a trim, seaworthy craft owned by the Grenfell Mission. Off to port, only vaguely visible, were the jagged, black Labrador mountains. The rest of the world was scintillant, every bit of it—with stars above, with reflections of stars on the surface of the smooth ground swells, with phosphorescent jellyfishes that looked like stars, down, down, perhaps a full fathom down, in the obsidian-clear water.

I was assisting W. E. Clyde Todd, veteran ornithologist of the Carnegie Museum in Pittsburgh, with his study of Labrador birds. I had seen Battle Harbor, Indian Harbor, Mugford Tickle, the Bishop's Mitre, Cape White Handkerchief, the Kiglipaits. For the first time in my life I had observed razor-billed auks, black guillemots, puffins, and glaucous gulls on their breeding grounds. I had been drawing these birds daily, usually from freshly shot specimens. Some day, I kept promising myself, I would study all these birds on my own; some day I would know them well. When I returned to the United States that fall, I was hopelessly in love with the North Country.

Small wonder that I went back, time after time: in 1923 to James Bay, via the Abitibi and Moose rivers; in 1926 as far as Richmond Gulf on the east coast of Hudson Bay and thence in a powered schooner that, having lost her propeller off Wolstenholme, was obliged to sail around almost the whole of the Labrador Peninsula in getting home; in 1928 to the north shore of the Gulf of Saint Lawrence. All of these trips I made with Mr. Todd, as his assistant.

In 1928 a chance meeting with a man named Sam G. Ford changed the very character of my life. Sam Ford knew Eskimos who themselves had seen nests of the *khavik*, the blue goose. For me the very words "blue goose" were a challenge. The fact that this fine species' nest and eggs had never been discovered had since the days of my boyhood been almost more than I could bear. When Sam Ford told me of the blue goose nests the Eskimos had found near a place called Cape Kendall, I could almost see the creamy-white eggs. It was as if they had suddenly come within touching distance.

So off I went for a year on Southampton Island, a 39,000-square-mile chunk of rock on which the Hudson's Bay Company had established a trading post only a few years before. Flying to the Arctic was unheard of in those days. I boarded the *Nascopie* at Montreal in July, disembarked a month later, and by midwinter was part of an amazing world of Eskimos, husky dogs, long trap lines, and nights so clear that the stars seemed to tinkle. *Tinkle,* not *twinkle.* Those stars flashed as if hung on wires and moved by the wind; the sharp sounds of weeds rustling and of ice crystals striking the hard snow seemed to come from them. Radio messages at Christmas informed me that the blue goose nest had already been found by Dewey Soper at Lake Amadjuak, in southwestern Baffin Island, but by this time I was beyond being disheartened. I had found a new self. Discovering undreamed of inner resources could, I decided, be just as important as discovering the nesting ground of a bird.

During the busy weeks following that long, wonderful winter, I painted birds like mad. I recall an art exhibit we had at the trading post. Tommy Bluce, a fine hunter of the Aivilik tribe, expressed his approval by picking gently at one picture with his thumbnail, as if trying to lift a feather. Shoofly, the oldest woman of the island and a veritable matriarch, did not realize that she could ruin a painting by handling it with oily fingers—but handle and ruin it she did. Oh, those were the days!

After my return to the States in the fall of 1930, my study of Arctic birds became methodical. I read widely, built up an extensive bibliography, and wrote a detailed account of the birdlife of Southampton Island. In 1931 I went north again—this time to the mouth of the Churchill River on the west coast of Hudson Bay, there to take part in discovering the nest and eggs of the Harris's Sparrow. In 1932, with Mr. Todd once more, I went to the Last Mountain Lake region of Saskatchewan. In 1934, I went to British Columbia with John B. Semple. Wherever I went, I drew birds. I had quite a collection of paintings by this time, most of them showing northern birds' heads and feet.

Foreword | ix

Then came World War II, a desire to be of use to my country, a strange dream called Officers' Training School, and a period of temporary duty in Alaska. Orders took me to the western end of the Aleutian Chain, where I met Rolly Wilson. Rolly and I, determined to obtain a specimen of the big leucosticte, or rosy finch, of those parts, almost put our shoulders out of joint throwing snowballs at rosy finches. Be it recorded that we came very close to hitting one or two of the birds. I made no paintings on Attu. No time for them.

During World War II, I became well acquainted with many remarkable men, among them Sir Hubert Wilkins and Vilhjalmur Stefansson. Friendship with Sir Hubert reached a climax when, while testing life-raft equipment in Casco Cove, we timed the dives of oldsquaw ducks. As for Stefansson, whom we all called "Stef," the friendship led to my preparing, at his request, the ornithological part of his Encyclopedia Arctica, a several-volume work most of which has not yet been published. Amassing this material reminded me continually of the magnum opus I wanted so much to write.

In the fall of 1952, "Stef" urged me to publish my material separately, in advance of the rest of his encyclopedia. But when I went over my manuscript, I found not only that it was badly out of date but that it revealed an appalling lack of firsthand knowledge concerning the Old World Arctic—especially Siberia.

In the summer of 1953 I had the pleasure of showing the Arctic to one of my most gifted graduate students, David F. Parmelee. Dave and I lived at the United States Air Force Base at the head of Frobisher Bay. We walked great distances daily observing several pairs of snowy owls at their nests. From time to time we took trips to far places—to Silliman's Fossil Mount by canoe with Robert Van Norman and Robert Pilot of the Royal Canadian Mounted Police, and to Wordie Bay, Cape Dorchester, and Lake Amadjuak by air with stouthearted personnel of the Royal Canadian Air Force.

My plan for getting to Siberia never seemed to resolve itself. I saved money, I wrote letters to ornithologists in Russia, I bought the six-volume work *Ptitzy Sovetskogo Soyuza* and studied the maps therein assiduously. My friend Gerhard Wiens translated certain passages for me and gave me a copy of the Russian alphabet. But I never went so far as to lay a plan before our Department of State.

Then, in the fall of 1957, came a letter from my old friend Olin Sewall Pettingill, Jr., to the effect that he and his wife were planning to go to Iceland the following summer. It would be fine if I came along. They had corresponded with Dr. Finnur Gudmundsson, the director of the Museum of Natural History in Reykjavík; they had ordered supplies and been promised the use of a Chevrolet panel truck. All I needed to do was make plane reservations, buy some field clothes, and arrange for someone to mow my yard. Iceland would be a step in the right direction—a step toward Siberia. I would take my paints along. I decided to go.

Not once during our eventful summer together did I think of writing a book about Iceland. I wrote notes daily, as has long been my custom. I painted regularly, as a rule using living birds as models. But the more I saw of Iceland the more interested I became in the island itself, the country as a governmental unit, the people. The vigor, resourcefulness, and independent spirit of the Icelanders impressed me tremendously.

Foreword | xi

When I returned to the United States in mid-August, I went straight to the home of my sister Evie in New York. A family get-together was going on. Father, remarkably hale for a man ninety years old, his wife, Anne, my sisters Dorothy and Evie, Evie's husband, Dr. Harry Swartz, and their twelve-year-old son Mark were having a reunion. Conversation with these six alert, well-informed persons convinced me that I should write a book about Iceland.

"How can you remember all those strange words?" asked sister Dot as I, showing my water-color drawings, used the Icelandic names for the birds. "Because I made a point of learning those bird names well. Aren't the words beautiful?" I countered. "Don't you agree?"

Off we went into an hour-long discussion of the Icelandic language. I realized full well how little I knew about the subject. I could tell my hearers that Icelandic as it is used today is close to the original Norwegian on which modern Norwegian is based, but that was about as far as I could go. Despite my ignorance, however, I knew more than the family did, and I could enlarge at great length about what I did know.

So it went concerning all manner of things Icelandic— the country's history, its sagas, its fishing, the remarkable bookstores in Reykjavík, the eiderdown industry, the steam jets, the boiling mudpots, the earthquakes and volcanoes, the sheep on the mountainsides, the glaciers, the waterfalls, the birch trees, the gorgeous pansies, the old cemetery near the unbelievably modern apartment house in which we all lived in Reykjavík, Finnur Gudmundsson and his family, Árni Waag and his family, Páll Steingrímsson and his family, the wonderful little archipelago known as the Vestmannaeyjar. Toward midnight I was hoarse; but never had I had a more sincerely interested audience.

As I thought about my book—the order in which I would present my material, the ground I would cover—I thrilled as I imagined the good I might do in taking Iceland's side with regard to fishing rights; in discussing the unfortunate black market, which had me feel like a heel every time I had exchanged American dollars for more Icelandic *krónur* than I had a right to receive; in writing frankly about Communism and the Soviet influence; in giving my own slant on the island's history, its remarkable literature, the fine university at Reykjavík, the problem of the United States military base at Keflavík, and so on. But when I tackled these matters, I almost instantly felt that I was beyond my depth and that what I wanted to say, what I really wanted to tell, was the simple story of a memorable summer.

I want to thank Finnur Gudmundsson for his careful checking of factual matter, spelling, and accents; the Pettingills for their sympathetic reading of the first draft; Sewall Pettingill for his graciousness in letting me use eight of his magnificent photographs as illustrations; Páll Steingrímsson for his comments on the chapter about the Vestmannaeyjar; Patricia K. Hill and Mont Muldrow for assistance in copying my execrable longhand; and Mrs. F. Ann Bernabe for preparing the final typescript. My railroad fare to New York and return was paid by the Faculty Research Fund of the University of Oklahoma. I might never have received this financial help had it not been for the interest of my friend Professor Duane H. D. Roller.

Norman, Oklahoma GEORGE MIKSCH SUTTON
February 21, 1961

Contents

Illustrations

Photographs

Iceland Summer

ADVENTURES OF A BIRD PAINTER

I

Can This Be Iceland?

My room in Reykjavík was the last straw. It was all that
was needed to prove that every idea I had entertained about
Iceland was wrong. I had read that Reykjavík was a fine,
modern city of seventy thousand; I knew perfectly well that
Icelanders were not acculturated Eskimos; I knew from con-
versations with my friend Professor Halldór Hermannsson
at Cornell University that the Icelandic literature was vast
and important. But despite all this I had envisioned Iceland
as a bleak, wind-torn, volcano-scourged wilderness. I had
half-believed that the people of Reykjavík lived in sod houses
or caves.

The room had been reserved for me by Finnur Gudmunds-
son, the director of the Museum of Natural History. When
I arrived in Reykjavík on June 10, Dr. Gudmundsson was in
Finland, but his secretary, a pretty young matron named
Gudrún Thorbergsdóttir, took me to see the room. We had

to walk only a block or so from the museum. The room was on the third floor of one of the new apartment buildings on Birkimelur, Street of Birches. The two big windows, handsomely curtained with lace, opened north and strong clear light poured in. "Elegant" was the word. Every bit of furniture was obviously an antique except for the neat built-in closets and drawers lining the west wall. To get into the room two keys were needed—one for the outside door downstairs, one for the apartment. The apartment door opened into a spacious hall at the end of which was a large bathroom.

My landlady-to-be, tall, gray-haired, stately Sigrídur Einarsdóttir, had been told that I was a reputable American who planned to study Icelandic birds all summer. She seemed satisfied with my appearance, produced a card table which I would need for my painting work, and listened carefully as I told her that I usually wore field clothes, that my comings and goings would be irregular, that I might be away for weeks at a stretch, that I probably would be skinning birds as well as painting them from time to time in the room. Sigrídur Einarsdóttir spoke English well and seemed to understand my every word. What she did not fully realize was that my heart was set on painting direct from living models whenever possible; that this would entail bringing the cheeping, squawking, quacking creatures indoors; that some of the dead specimens would smell bad, and so on. I suppose I should have explained all this in vivid detail, but I was more than eager to get settled, and I made a firm inner resolve to keep the noise to a minimum and to spread newspapers without fail over the oriental rug. Sigrídur Einarsdóttir did not welcome me effusively. She may have had misgivings. But she had told Finnur Gudmundsson that this room would be available. So, for better or for worse, it was mine.

Sigrídur Einarsdóttir showed Gudrún Thorbergsdóttir and me the rest of her apartment. The brief look we had at tapestries, oil paintings, and carved furniture was enough to convince me that this woman had created here her own little center of beauty and culture. She explained that I was welcome to use her sitting room for my painting work whenever she was not there. Pointing to the kitchen, she made clear that I could brew coffee should I wish to. She showed me where my towels would be in the bathroom, explained how the window latches worked. "The keys," said she, "are important. I am not often here. I work all day at the telephone company. You have two keys. I have two keys. If you lose your keys and I cannot be found, the Fire Department will have to let you in. That happened to me once. They got in through a window I always leave unlocked. They had to use the long ladders." I gave the keys a pinch, to be sure they were there. "Now the telephone," she continued. "You will take it from the hall to your room when you receive a call. It plugs in at the end of the couch. I do not want to hear a word you say." This pronouncement gave me a start. What on earth might I be saying that would be unfit for this handsome, well-groomed daughter of a viking to hear?

I lugged my bags up the stairs and invited Gudrún Thorbergsdóttir to have luncheon with me. Going to a restaurant would give me a further look at the city, it would put some of my newly acquired Icelandic *krónur* (money) to work, and besides I was hungry. Breakfast on the plane had been unconscionably early—and sketchy. "How do I call a taxi?" I asked, glancing at the phone. "We will walk," answered

Gudrún Thorbergsdóttir. "I like to walk. I walk all the time."

We walked back to the museum and started for Gildas-kálinn, a restaurant in the heart of the business district. The sun was bright, the air sharp. I could have got along without a coat, but was glad I had one on. In the big cemetery to our left stood birch trees twenty feet high, and I could see that there were good-sized trees all about us. Bright flowers were blooming everywhere—anemones, larkspur, and the most glorious pansies I had ever seen. A luxuriant shrub used frequently as a hedge proved to be a gooseberry, but the berries had not yet formed. The well-paved street led down a slope, then alongside Tjörnin, a big lake whose surface was so still that every building on the opposite side was mirrored perfectly. On the shore were literally hundreds of ducks. I could see that most of these were mallards and I assumed, from their docility, that they were of a domestic strain. A noise startled some of them, and off they flew. They were wild birds, every one of them, but so long had they been treated well, so long had they been fed by everyone, that they had become remarkably confiding. Out a way, not quite so sure of themselves as the mallards, were drake and hen widgeons, pintails, gadwalls, and a drake teal, resplendent in the bright light. The widgeons were of the Old World species, of course, a species I had seen only once in America; the teal looked for all the world like an American green-winged teal, but it had no white mark on the side of its chest. A few of the hen mallards had chicks. One hen, flattened out on the grassy bank, let us approach to within five or six feet. As we drew slowly closer and stretched out a hand, she raised her head feathers, quacked loudly, and slid into the water, suddenly becoming thirteen birds instead of one. Her ducklings were tiny fluffs, but they paddled swiftly in her wake as if they had known how to paddle for years.

On an islet well out from shore a pair of mute swans were nesting. This species was not native to Iceland; the truly Icelandic swans were whoopers. On another islet arctic terns and black-headed gulls were settled for the summer. At the water's edge I saw my first white wagtail—a dainty gray, black, and white bird with a long tail that wagged not from side to side but up and down. It was gathering mouthfuls of midges which it carried to a nest near one of the houses.

Luncheon was excellent, especially the soup, which was served in a large tureen. Finished with one bowlful, we ladled out another. I could not have had a more pleasant companion than Gudrún Thorbergsdóttir.

"When will Dr. Gudmundsson be back?" I asked. "Oh, surely within a very few days," came the prompt reply. "But I believe the Pettingills will get here before he does. Remember, you can have the truck whenever you want it. It's parked right there at the museum."

II

Introductions: A Pipit Surprise

SEWALL PETTINGILL AND HIS WIFE, ELEANOR, were good friends from Maine who had come to Iceland in early May, who had a room on the second floor of the same apartment building as mine, and who were now in Finland, attending an international ornithological congress. They had been hard at work making a color film dealing with Icelandic bird life. They had spent much of their time at Thingeyri in northwestern Iceland, in the very heart of the great fjord-indented peninsula known as Vestfjardakjálkinn, photographing eider ducks. One pair had consisted of a king eider drake and a common eider hen. Such interbreeding of the two species had been reported, but never, so far as we could ascertain, photographed. As a rule the king eider did not nest in Iceland; it was a more or less regular winter visitor.

I was sorry the Pettingills were away, but glad for the chance to become acquainted with Reykjavík on my own.

I looked upon the panel truck mentioned by Gudrún with disfavor at the moment. It was a thing of many and unpredictable gears. I had started it and, deafened by the grinding roar, had backed into and almost across the street before I realized which way I was going. In Iceland one kept to the left in driving. That I could remember. One had also to bear in mind whether one intended to go forward or backward. Learning to do the correct thing with this truck, which I naturally called "Big Blue," was an ordeal I would put off as long as possible. Just now I would walk. What I craved was the natural, the easy, the untechnological approach to Iceland.

So, in woolen shirt and with binocular, I set out afoot for the low-lying treeless country between the edge of the city and the airport. This area looked wild from the taxi, but part of it proved to be a series of vaguely marked-off garden plots through which deep drainage ditches ran. The soil was black and wet despite the unusual dryness of the season. In the untilled areas the grass was luxuriant, much of it knee high. A bit taller than the grass were scattered dead stalks of dock. A short scouring-rush or horsetail grew in the shallow water of the ditches. Clumps of bright yellow flowers proved to be marsh marigolds.

I was astounded by the abundance of birds. The farther I walked, the more of them there seemed to be. In a barren spot not far from the highway a pair of ringed plovers called excitedly, letting me know clearly enough that they had eggs or chicks there. Along the main ditch lived two or three pairs of white wagtails. I followed one pair about, watched them carry load after load of food to the farther bank, and finally discovered the nest, six or eight feet down from the top and

Introductions: A Pipit Surprise / 9

well hidden by shaggy grass. In it were several tiny young. A wholly new bird for me was the redwing—not the red-winged blackbird of America, of course, but a thrush which reminded me strongly, the moment I saw it, of a friendly, plump, American robin. This redwing, oddly enough, had no red on its wings, but a large spot of reddish brown marked each side or flank. A pair of redwings had a nest somewhere among the garden plots, but I failed to find it.

There were two ways of crossing the big main ditch— walking a considerable distance to a plank bridge, or clambering down the almost vertical twelve-foot bank, wading the stream, and climbing the other bank. The latter method wasn't easy, and it meant getting muddy. Beyond the main ditch there were no garden plots. Here, in a world of lush grass, lived redshanks, common snipes, meadow pipits, and golden plovers, not to mention the hen mallards, which seemed to have nests all over the place. As I entered this verdant world, I found it hard to believe that it was inhabited by anything aside from the redshanks, for assuredly they were among the noisiest, most assertive birds I had ever observed. In yelping pairs they flew to meet me. Wherever I went they accompanied me, calling incessantly. A great deal of white showed in their wings. Occasionally, in moments of ecstasy, they discontinued their perfunctory yammering, flew upward gracefully on quivering wings, and gave forth a lively, jolly-sounding, strongly rhythmical *til-willy, til-willy, til-willy*, over and over and over, almost exactly the sort of performance one would expect from a willet in America.

Almost as active as the redshanks were the snipes, which by this time were flying about madly, some far above ground, others low, giving forth that weirdly beautiful windy sound which may be called hooting, for want of a better word. Careful observers believe that this hooting is produced not by any part of the snipe's vocal apparatus but by the rapidly vibrating widespread tail feathers, and I must say that as the snipes passed over me I clearly saw, through the glass, that their tails were fanned out extraordinarily. Repeatedly I received the impression that the birds were diving straight at me; and thrilling it was to hear the hooting of an approaching bird, to watch it as it grew larger and larger, then changed course abruptly and towered so swiftly that in a matter of seconds it was a tiny point of black racing across the sky.

So deeply did I enjoy the snipes that I couldn't quite forgive the redshanks for their tiresome scolding, but my ears had a way of disregarding that which they did not particularly care for, and thus it was that, over and over, I caught snatches of the flight songs of a meadow pipit. This bird interested me especially, for I had become well acquainted with two other pipit species on their nesting grounds and I wanted to find out exactly how this unknown differed from the known. One fact about its behavior impressed me immediately: often it alighted on the vegetation, especially the tough tall stalks of dead dock. This was something I had never seen the Sprague's pipit or water pipit do in America. The meadow pipit's song was about what I had expected it to be—a monotonous, unmusical repetition of a note that was not even a whistle—but how the little bird gave itself to its singing!

A pipit surprise was in store for me. Just after finding and carefully marking a mallard's nest I was walking through some tall tufts of grass when out from underfoot flew a pipit. I knew what it was, for it was brown and its tail flashed white, and I knew there was a nest, for only a nesting bird would risk its life in that way. I had very nearly stepped on it. I parted the grass with my hands and there, in a deep, beautifully lined cup, were the six dark eggs.

The golden plovers were not in pairs. They were in loose flocks, feeding peacefully on well-drained slopes where the grass was thin and not very high. Occasionally I heard a clear whistle from them as they took flight. Obviously they were not nesting close by.

III

Off in a Jeep

NEXT MORNING I JUMPED out of bed annoyed with myself for having wasted so much wonderful daylight. It was a quarter to five o'clock, yet the sun had been bright for a long time. I had not yet adjusted to the almost continuous midsummer daylight of this boreal part of the world.

Not liking instant coffee very well and not wanting to make a noise in the kitchen, I decided to explore the city for an all-night coffee shop. I wanted to know the whereabouts of such places and I was eager to learn more about Reykjavík and its people.

The morning could not have been lovelier. As I walked past the cemetery with its neat, walled-in plots, its incredible flowers, its caroling redwings, and the strange, strange names on the stones, I realized that I was beginning to feel a genuine affection for Iceland. I'd hardly met anyone yet. I had no idea whether Americans were liked or disliked in this country. But there was an abiding dignity here, a fearless acceptance of both the bitter and the sweet, a willingness to work, a fierce love of homeland. I felt it all as I walked past stone after stone, then down the hill to Tjarnargata, the street bordering the lake. Was I homesick for Oklahoma and Nebraska and West Virginia, or had full realization that certain feelings are universal all at once been too much for me?

The slant red sunlight made brilliant the varicolored buildings, the treetops, the glossy green heads of the mallard drakes. On my way along one side of the big square, past the Parliament Building and the old Lutheran cathedral, I did not meet a soul.

"No," said the young woman at the desk of the Hotel Borg, "the dining room will not be open until eight." My next question had to do with the acceptability of field attire. Doing her best to avoid discomfiting me, but sensing that her decision might establish a dangerous precedent, she sized me up swiftly. Her exact words didn't matter; the look on her face told me that though I'd not be turned away I'd be a shade more welcome dressed a shade more formally. This was my first lesson in Icelandic propriety.

The coffee shop the young woman told me about was just around the corner, on the street called Laekjargata. It was open. Indeed, it was going strong. Here I encountered utter inability to understand English. Not with all the sign language at my command could I put across the idea of bacon and eggs. A rather severe, well-dressed young male customer came to my aid. Through him I learned that bacon and eggs would not be served before eight o'clock.

So I had coffee and a slice of cake, and for the next half-

STRAUMÖND

Female harlequin duck
caught in a net hung under a bridge over the Laxá River
near Mývatn, northeastern Iceland.
Painted direct from life June 20, 1958.

Oystercatcher chick painted direct from life
June 13, 1958, at Seltjarnarnes,
near Reykjavík, Iceland.

hour I enjoyed myself hugely. All the customers were men, and in general they were a hearty, weathered, unshaven lot, many of them fresh in from a voyage. Some had been drinking. They did not go storming about threatening to wreck the place, but they did occasionally become loud-mouthed and argumentative to the point of pounding the table, upsetting coffee, and scuffling. The waitresses evinced no particular concern, for they had an efficient procedure whereby, with a wave of a little white towel from the front door, they summoned the police. The regular customers knew of the towel and watched it respectfully. Observant newcomers soon perceived that the towel was important. If a waitress with towel in hand moved ever so unostentatiously toward the door, decorum usually returned at once. But there were times when uninformed newcomers or inebriated regulars paid no attention to the towel and the police car drew up, burly officers came in, offenders were hustled out, and the restaurant became exceedingly quiet.

Coffee hour over, I walked fast to my special birding ground, watched the white wagtails a while, then found an extremely self-assured mallard and her nest. I was about to call her tame or confiding, but the connotation of those words is all wrong. When, almost trod upon, she fluttered off a way, she was not in the least demure. She was angry. She had only three eggs, but these she valued highly, so back she came to strike at my shoes with her wings, to hiss loudly, and to bite my fingers when I tried to stroke her. She was by far the fiercest hen mallard I had ever seen. In her nest again, she refused to settle down while I was within touching distance. With every move I made she hissed. When I knelt beside her and did my best to talk her into accepting me, she fluffed out her plumage and lunged at me. So I moved back. When I was four feet away she shut her bill and a tolerant expression spread over her face. *What a marvellous chance to do a direct-from-life drawing,* thought I. *I'll go back for my outfit right now, and may the good Lord grant us more of this dry weather!*

At the room I found a note to the effect that Árni Waag had been calling on the telephone, that he would call again that evening. Árni was one of Iceland's leading amateur ornithologists. I wanted very much to meet him. The Pettingills had told me of him, cautioning me that his first name was pronounced not *Arney,* but *Owt-ny.*

I was thumbtacking paper to a drawing board when the phone rang. It was Árni. He was elated, jubilant, beside himself, for he had obtained the use of a jeep and could spend the whole afternoon showing me birds. Never was I given a warmer welcome. He would come by soon to pick me up.

By the time that afternoon was over I felt that I must surely have seen most of Iceland. We visited a cemetery where, in thick, low conifers, I inspected redwing nests Árni had been observing. At a plantation of birches and "Alaska spruces" we found more redwing nests and caught a baby redwing that looked so much like a baby American robin I could scarcely believe my eyes. Off we rushed to a lake about which there were dunlins, red-necked (northern) phalaropes, Slavonian (horned) grebes, and whooper swans. "We will look for duck nests," suggested Árni. As we zigzagged across the spongy ground, we were followed by a band of small, furry, sweet-faced horses that wanted so to be petted that they nudged us when we paid no attention to them. We had not time enough to walk round the lake, but I made a point of standing still a while listening to the trilling of the dunlins. How the delightful sound carried me back to places I knew well in our American Arctic, to the tundra country in which *our* dunlin lived! Only we called our dunlin the red-backed sandpiper.

Off we went, following the rough road into wilder, ever wilder country. At a lake deep-set in lava rock we came upon a small flock of whimbrels, large shore birds with long de-curved bills. Mentioning merlins, Árni headed the jeep across country, Oklahoma fashion, and we spent a hair-raising half-hour wandering in and out of canyons following what appeared to be sheep trails. Finally, greatly to my relief, the jeep stopped and we got out. I followed Árni to a half-dome of lava, and there, sure enough, the merlins were. The male came to meet us on rapidly beating wings, squealing shrilly. As we climbed the acclivity on the far side of the half-dome, the female left the eyrie, which was not on a ledge but in a shadowy, moss-lined crevice. Up the all but perpendicular slope Árni climbed as easily, it seemed to me, as if he'd been walking upstairs. The three eggs were rusty brown. Those wonderful little falcons: how I loved their trim compactness, their speed, their wild squealing!

The merlin habitat was by far the wildest country I had thus far seen in Iceland. Everything aside from the sky was dark brown, black in the shadows, treeless, virtually birdless. On our way from the jeep to the eyrie and back we saw only one bird aside from the merlins—a raven. Árni informed me that the merlins often traveled a long way for food. They lived principally on meadow pipits.

We went through Hafnarfjördur, a neat, brightly painted fishing village, on our way to an arctic tern colony. At the edge of the village were great racks of drying codfish—probably bound for Nigeria. We stopped for a while to watch some men cutting up and burying a huge shark. This would, when properly mellowed, be dug up and consumed, with *aquavit*.

The tern colony surprised me in that it was not at all near water. It was on a high barren slope overlooking, but fully a mile from, the sea. The terns dived at us savagely and, I add with chagrin, whitewashed us. Not far from the terns Árni showed me a snow bunting nest he had been visiting. Alas, it had been despoiled, possibly by a mink. Minks were not native to Iceland, of course, but a population had established itself and spread widely within recent years, winning for itself the cordial hatred of all Icelanders.

Árni wanted me to see another tern colony. This was on flat, low-lying ground close to the ocean and near the famous Bessastadir, the home of the President of Iceland. I was struck with the bold, clean-cut beauty of the great house. The colony was remarkable in that it was so mixed. Among the hundreds of terns were many pairs of black-headed gulls —a species which had only recently invaded Iceland from the Continent; wherever we walked we flushed hen eiders from their down-lined nests, and all about us grazed placid cows. The cows puzzled me. Some of them looked enough like Guernseys to make me fairly certain that they were of that persuasion. "What about these cows, Árni? Are they Guernseys?" The question should never have been asked. Árni gave me a defiant, uncompromising, almost hostile look. "They are Iceland cows," he said. "Iceland!" I had touched that which had kept his country together these one thousand years; that which had won for it its independence; that which had kept its language pure; that which had engendered its remarkable literature. I had learned another lesson in propriety. Guernseys would not be mentioned again.

On our way back to Reykjavík, Árni pointed out great cement tanks in which the city's hot water was stored. Already I had learned something about that water. The first time I had drawn a bath I had waited a long time for the water to become hot; the second time, assuming that it would be cold or tepid, I had given myself a mild scalding.

IV

A Very Full Day

THURSDAY, JUNE 12, was cloudy and raw. I put on my hunting coat, wrapped drawing board and paints in a waterproof cloth, and set out for the ill-tempered mallard. On my way I stopped for a bite of breakfast at my café on Laekjargata.

The restaurant was busier and much noisier than usual. A waitress I had not seen before was having trouble with a customer who, outspoken in his admiration for her, pinched her when opportunity offered. The noise subsided slightly as I wandered about with my tray, looking for an unoccupied table; but once I had sat down conversation regained its fervor. The several men at one long table were particularly loud-mouthed, and I noticed that some statements, whatever their meaning, were accompanied by hair rumpling. Occasionally, to my surprise, I heard good English, but this came not from the table just mentioned but from a far corner. Here a quarrel seemed to be brewing. The English words came clearly now, "If you can't speak Icelandic so people can understand you, why don't you speak your own language? You're Welsh, you say. Well, then, speak Welsh!" I'd have given a good deal to see just who had been speaking Icelandic badly and who my own tongue. But I decided against changing my position lest I miss something interesting in another part of the room.

I perceived that one waitress had her eye on the little white towel. Suddenly, the police car passed. It did not stop, it did not even slow up, but the quiet that descended was like that of the forest when the hawk sails over. The party from the Welshman's corner walked out, soberly enough. I could not tell which man had spoken English. I felt a little let down as they departed.

An argument started at the noisy table. This time someone was dealt a resounding whack and the waitress started briskly for the towel. Her move was followed immediately, long before the towel reached the door, by the decorous departure of five customers. The "goodly crowd" was thinning.

The towel was not waved. The obstreperous element had, it seemed, been eliminated. But no one needed to remind me that the potential remaining was terrific. Suddenly a man at the erstwhile noisy table looked hard at me, rose, and started toward me. This put me in a quandary. I knew he was far younger and stronger than I. What if he started an argument about capitalism and became angry because I could not speak Icelandic? What if he said something like "All you Americans ought to pick yourselves and your Air Force Base up and go home"?

Well, said I to myself, this is no time for faintheartedness. Let him come. Let him argue. I've seen many a movie in which someone hits someone else effectively with a chair. He came straight on, put a hand on my shoulder, leaned down so that I could not miss a syllable, and said, in an entirely agreeable voice, "Good morning!"

When, half an hour later, I greeted the hen mallard with the same two words, her reply was a hiss. Nor could I so much as touch her without making her furious. When I tried stroking her head, she gave my fingers a funny, exploratory nibble with her harmless beak.

I heaped grass about four feet from the nest, sat on this improvised cushion and started drawing, but soon realized that the wind was strong and the air chilly. I had supposed that my model would stay put once she had become accustomed to me, but the sound of my eraser annoyed her and she scuttled off in a huff, turned when a yard or so away, hissed loudly at me with head held low, and returned by a back route, slipping through the grass with astonishing speed and noiselessness. When she settled down, her flank feathers were rumpled, so I tried smoothing them into place. This she would not tolerate, so, failing once more to scare me with nibbling, she ran off again. Suddenly the sun came out and the whiteness of the paper blinded me. When my eyes returned to normal, and I could see that my model was once more on her eggs, the brightness faded and the rain started. I covered the drawing hastily with the waterproof. The sun returned soon and the rain stopped, but there was no denying the fact that I had become chilly. The duck now seemed to forget all about me and turned her eggs with her bill. When she resumed incubation she was in a wholly new position. I penciled in some grass blades swiftly. When it began sprinkling again, I decided that the fates were against me. After wrapping my gear carefully, I swung my arms about fiercely, trying to warm up. I was stiff and miserable with the cold.

While, hour after hour, I had been sitting there, the several redshanks of the vicinity had come to accept me as part of their habitat. Now, as I prepared to depart, I noticed that the meadow was remarkably quiet. I happened to be standing still when a redshank flew out of the deep grass about forty paces away. The fact that it did not call impressed me instantly, but I did not think about the matter until a moment later, when *two* redshanks bore down upon me fairly shrieking their annoyance. With habit born of experience, I had noted the exact spot from which the single bird had risen. Running to this spot immediately, parting the grass with care, and searching as only a determined bird student can search under such circumstances, I found the four big eggs. They were brownish olive, spotted with dark brown. The grass had covered them completely. Never in the world would I have found them had I not happened to see the bird fly up. It was the only redshank's nest any of us saw that whole summer.

Before the morning was over I found a common snipe's nest, too. The snipe flew up well ahead of me, but I could tell from the way it spread its tail as it hesitated in midair, then feigned slight injury as it made off, that there was something out of the ordinary about its departure. There were three eggs. How lucky I had been to find these nests! How pleased the Pettingills would be.

As if I hadn't already had a pretty full day, Árni Waag appeared at seven o'clock that evening and off we went, this time in "Big Blue," to birding grounds several kilometers south of the city. Árni did the driving. Following the dusty, much used Sudurlandsvegur, the main highway, we presently found ourselves on a side road in a low-lying marshy area in which whimbrels, golden plovers, dunlins, and red-necked phalaropes were preparing to nest. By this time it was raining. The parched countryside needed the drenching. We drove farther, through oddly shaped masses of black lava, to a big lake in which there were scaup ducks, teal, and whooper swans. The scaups were of the species we called the greater scaup in America. With two of the whoopers were four gray cygnets. In a marsh near the lake was a wholly new bird for me, a black-tailed godwit. It stood about as high as a whimbrel, but had a long, very slightly upturned yellow bill. Not far from the godwit, in a gravelly flat, two oystercatchers must have had a nest or brood. The big, boldly black and white birds had orange-scarlet bills. Their principal cry was a loud *peep* or *keep*.

On our way back to Reykjavík I had my first taste of driving and my second round with "Big Blue." Keeping to the left of the highway wasn't as difficult as I'd expected it would be.

———————————————∨———————————————

V

The Summer Truly Begins

IT WASN'T QUITE RAINING the following morning, but the sky was gray and the wind raw. Wearing a heavy shirt, hunting coat, and rubber boots and carrying my painting outfit, I followed the coffee route to the dour mallard hen and set to work. This time I dealt with my model objectively, addressing her in a matter-of-fact voice and slapping her when she hissed. She would not leave the nest. One of her eggs was pipping.

I plied pencil and brush for all I was worth, but it was a losing battle. My hands grew numb; I could not keep them flexible. The wind was relentless. The duck would not stay still. To give myself a rest from the problems of plumage pattern, I worked at plant detail—but alas, I seemed to get nowhere. After about four hours of trying, I gave up. The drawing has not been finished to this day.

I decided to cache my belongings and visit the several

nests I had found. At the redshank's nest I might easily have caught the bird had I known it was there. I walked up casually, knelt as I started to part the grass, and up the redshank fluttered into my very face. The nest was deep, the grass so thick that the bird could not possibly have run off through it.

Not a nest I knew about in that area had come to grief. This was a surprise, for nests near trading posts and Eskimo encampments in the American Arctic are so apt to be destroyed by half-starved dogs that a bird student can consider himself lucky if he does not lose in this way half the nests he finds. In Iceland there seemed to be no dogs at all, and very few cats.

Word came that the Pettingills were to arrive late that evening. The news made it difficult for me to plan my work, but when Árni Waag proposed that we make a quick try for oystercatchers, I could not refuse him. "Why not get a baby oystercatcher? You can paint it, then come over to our house for supper. Later we can go to the airport to meet the Pettingills." The plan and invitation were far too attractive to turn down.

The oystercatchers Árni took me to lived out toward the farthest tip of Seltjarnarnes, a long, low, peninsula inhabited also by a huge colony of arctic terns and a few ringed plovers. Above the high-tide mark grew low, sprawling, greenish-gray plants whose blooms were heavenly blue, and tough grasses that looked like sea oats. The sand was fine and dark, basaltic sand, difficult to walk in, especially where it was dry. Well offshore, in the gray sea, floated ducks that looked like scaups, but their backs were black and a long crest hung down from the back of each glossy black head. They were tufted ducks, the first I had seen in Iceland.

26 / *The Summer Truly Begins*

We found only a few scattered pairs of oystercatchers, but the stocky, pied birds were much in evidence from the moment we invaded their nesting ground until we departed. Hoping to obtain a newly hatched chick—the plumage stage I especially wanted—we sat down and watched the old birds patiently from what we considered inconspicuous positions; we hid behind piles of kelp or among the sea oats; we wandered about as if wholly disinterested—in short, we did everything we could think of to throw those noisy, stubborn birds off their guard, but never did they trust us. As a rule they were easy to see. Often they almost threw themselves at us, crossing and recrossing in front of us. But occasionally they alighted out of sight beyond a ridge of sand, sneaked back quickly so as not to lose sight of us, and crouched, exposing only the very tops of their heads and their bright red eyes. So it went for about two hours. Árni and I, each somewhat annoyed with himself, separated—he going farther out the peninsula, I ensconcing myself in the remains of an old ship.

For a time I was hopeful. I could look out through cracks and portholes and between planks piled above the hatch. Two oystercatchers flew off and the peeping stopped. I watched the birds until they alighted, a hundred yards away. I expected one of them to run straight to a nest, but they both stood there, doing not a thing. Then, to my utter disgust, I found that two more birds, standing behind a heap of kelp near the ship, with only their heads showing, were eyeing me suspiciously. If I so much as wiggled a finger at them from above the pile of planks, they began their shrill peeping. For all I know they had seen *me* through the cracks and portholes that I had been considering solely mine.

Suddenly I heard a shout. The triumphant Árni, charging toward me with his curly hair wildly blowing, had in his hand a downy chick, gray as basaltic sand on its upper parts, white as snow on its belly. Sure enough, it was an oyster-catcher! It was very young, of precisely the age I needed for my painting. We were so excited we could hardly talk.

In haste we drove back to Birkimelur. I painted furiously the rest of the afternoon, and at supper I was able to show Árni and his fine family my first completed drawing of an Iceland bird. The summer had truly begun. Never did I enjoy a meal more. The sausage, creamed potatoes, waffles, strawberry preserves, and coffee were delicious. Árni and I ate by ourselves at a small table beautifully set for two. Árni's wife kept an eye on us, making certain that there was no shortage of food. Part of my happiness stemmed from realization that I had at last painted something.

The Pettingills arrived on schedule. The three of us sat up late talking about the meeting they had attended, about Finland, about plans for the coming few days. We would not leave Reykjavík until after Independence Day, June 17. When we did leave, we would head northward and eastward for Mývatn, Midge Lake.

VI

A Disagreeable Fall

I WANTED VERY MUCH to show Sewall the nests I had found, but it was raining steadily next morning. I donned my big raincoat and walked to the cemetery to observe redwings. I found the adult males busy singing, the adult females on nests. The redwings which continued to fly along the path just ahead of me, and to hunt food assiduously among the flowers, were full-feathered young of first broods. I found two occupied nests—one, holding five eggs, in a birch; the other, brimming with four well-developed chicks, in a small spruce. These chicks would, I foresaw, be just right for painting within a day or two.

The redwings' songs were cheery and tuneful, but they did not—and this surprised me—remind me in the least of American robins' songs. The birds sang from the roofs of the big houses beyond Sudurgata, the street just south of the cemetery. The rain, far from silencing them, seemed to incite them to sing. The season had been very dry.

Small birds that I heard and saw repeatedly in the cemetery that morning of June 14 were redpolls. I had heard what I felt sure were redpoll call notes on my first day in Iceland, and a jubilant song high over the city on June 13 had called a redpoll to mind, but this time I saw the birds clearly. Moving about restlessly, they fed in the birches and larches. Two that allowed me to approach closely looked like sibling young of the year. Assuredly they had no pink at all on their breasts, and even when I looked at them closely through my binocular, I could see very little red in their crown plumage. Árni Waag had told me of seeing young redpolls out of the nest during the first few days of June.

The great surprise of the morning was a brambling, an Old World species that I had never seen before, which flew up in response to my continued "squeaking." The "squeaking" threw the adult redwings into paroxysms of rage; some young redwings flew up and looked at me inquiringly, but were obviously not much perturbed; the redpolls were agitated and uttered plaintive notes in addition to their customary *churrs*, but did not seem to be angered or frightened. All at once in flew this handsome new bird—conspicuously larger than the redpolls, black, white, and rich brown, with finchlike bill—a brambling. How sorry I was that Árni was not with me. This was obviously a fully adult male. Árni had seen a male in first breeding plumage several times on June 11.

The rain stopped by nine o'clock. After breakfast with the well-rested Pettingills I took Sewall to see my several nests, especially that of the white wagtail, a species he had been

SKÓGARTHRÖSTUR

Young redwing just after leaving the nest.
Painted direct from life
at Reykjavík, Iceland, June 16, 1958.

Common snipe chick about two days old.
Painted direct from life at Reykjavík,
Iceland, June 17, 1958.

keen to photograph. About half-past ten he returned to Birkimelur while I stayed afield hoping to find a baby snipe or redshank.

I was standing in the deep grass listening to the snipes when the thought crossed my mind that we had failed to examine the wagtail nest. We had watched the old birds for some time, to be sure, but we had not ascertained that the young were still in the nest. What if the brood had already fledged? I decided to return for a careful look. If the chicks were just about ready to leave, photographs should be taken immediately. I did not want to take a chick for my painting work until Sewall had obtained a good photographic record of the parent birds.

This decision to examine the nest, this overeagerness to make certain that we had not already delayed too long, might have cost me my life. I had placed a stake marker carefully at the top of the bank directly above the nest. All too hastily, all too confidently, and wholly forgetful of the recent rain, I climbed down a way from this marker, then jumped to a grassy tuft or knob I knew was just about at nest level.

The sudden impact dislodged the tuft, my feet caught in a crack of their own making, and down I pitched, arms and head first, to the bottom of the ditch, a shaggy mass of turf with me. There was neither clatter nor crash as I struck. My hands must have broken the fall, though a blow on the head dazed me momentarily. My face was in water about six inches deep. I tasted mud. As I lifted my head I realized that more earth was coming loose above and behind me, and that this was falling in heavy waves on my legs, hips, back, and shoulders. The sound of its reluctant breaking free and of its falling was vaguely like that of distant surf pounding. I sensed no pain, no pain at all. I was sure that no bones were broken. But never had I felt such weight, such inexorable heaviness.

The water near my face ran red, so I knew I had been cut somewhere. My hands, though perfectly free, were in water several inches deep. With one hand I snatched the binocular from my neck and saw that it was not damaged. My wrist watch, though wet, was running. Straining, I looked upward and backward. The wagtail's nest was rudely exposed; all the grass was gone from below and in front of it; but it was there, intact. One of the old birds was flitting about close by, its beak full of insects. The brood had not yet flown!

When I tried to pull myself out, I found I could lift my shoulders a little despite their soggy burden, that my arms were free, but that from the waist on I was pinned down. At the moment I could not see exactly what was holding me; but when I tried to lift my hips, to pull my knees forward, I realized that my right foot was twisted. Exploring with my hand, I found that loose earth on my neck came away easily. As the muddied water moved slowly off I wondered whether, impounded as it now might be, it presently would start to rise. That, I knew, could be bad.

All thought of calling for help I dismissed from mind after one brief, halfhearted shout. I knew that the sound had carried nowhere. My voice seemed to be pinned down along with the rest of me. Hringbraut, a much used highway, was only a couple of hundred yards away, but no one there could be expected to hear anything above the noise of traffic. No, getting out of this mess was my own affair. I had been in tough spots before. I would dig out somehow.

So dig I did. Between bouts I moved a mass of mud over

for a chin rest. This kept my mouth and nose above water without unduly tiring the neck muscles. Within half an hour —by the watch, now resting on a big clod—I raised myself from the waist up on my arms and saw that the stream was free to flow, that the water was not rising. The work was exhausting, for muscles of the hand and arms do not take kindly to continued activity behind one's back. Each time I tried to pull free, the twisted right leg was seized by a painful cramp. The mass of earth above my hips and legs was incredible. One great chunk, about twenty feet long and up to three feet thick, must have fallen all at once.

The surface earth was matted with tough rootlets. One handful that came away with surprising ease turned out to be a mass of coarse reddish-brown hair, possibly from a cow's tail. This hair gave me one of the strangest pangs I had ever experienced. For some unaccountable reason I decided that the hair must be my own; that it must have been scraped off my head during the fall. I felt of my scalp and was less surprised by finding half-dried blood there than by *not* finding a hairless spot. The thought that my hair was actually of that color and texture, that it had probably turned that way through neglect, that friends had never said a word about it —all this horrified me. Vanity, vanity, all indeed must be vanity. . . .

I realized, as handful after handful of earth came away, that I had been wonderfully lucky. Had the earth on my shoulders fallen on my head instead, had my arms not been free from the first, had I been knocked unconscious, I might by this time have been drowned. Realization that I was alive, fully alive, and that the water was not rising, filled me with more than hope; it filled me with an almost defiant gratitude.

A Disagreeable Fall / 33

No sky was more beautiful than that which I saw above me, no water ever clearer than that which ran past my face. The ditch did not seem hostile. The wagtails were no longer agitated. Often one came so close that I would not have been greatly surprised had it alighted on me. I noticed, with some surprise, that although the water seemed cold to my hands, I did not feel cold myself.

Digging became routine. The right hand worked a while, then had to rest. The left hand took over, then rested. The two hands could not work together. Meanwhile the brain darted thither and yon, dwelling for a time on the bold, stark beauty of Reykjavík; the thrill of being in Iceland; the mystery of such a friendship as that which had bound me all these years to Sewall Pettingill and to that beautiful, hard-working, straight-shooting Eleanor, his wife; the luck that had put me in quarters close to the museum, close to the lake, close even to this wild land, a bit of which was now holding me captive. How I had thrilled as I had seen my first redshank, the peaceful golden plovers, the bleating snipes, and those fragile, lovable little birds, the meadow pipits—all of them only a strone's throw from this very spot. This was not a bad place to be. Not a bad place really. I could hear the calls of all these birds now, every one of them if I listened carefully. A snipe was hooting loudly directly above me.

Dig, you fool. You'll have to dig harder if you're ever to get out of here! Remember what Árni said about Iceland weather—about how the sun shines one minute and the heavens open up the next? You're not out of this ditch yet, not by a long way. A sudden rain could mean a swift rise, perhaps a flood. The torrent might wash the dirt off you, but you might be a sorry corpse by that time. I had now been digging three-quarters of an hour. I lifted myself on my arms, pulled hard, felt a violent cramp in the right leg, and gladly let it slip back into place. I perspired a little from the pain.

More digging. More thinking. Thinking and remembering seemed to be such an easy, natural part of all this. I remembered a black and white bantam hen neighbors had given me when I was seven or eight years old, back in Nebraska; I remembered how I had thrown it into a pond to see if it could swim; how it had swum, unsteadily to be sure, but pretty well for a chicken; how I had taken it, soaking wet, to my mother, who, with infinite forbearance, had not chided me much but had put the hen near the oven and brought it back to life.

Dig, you fool. Dig harder. Stop the woolgathering and dig! The fingernails were wearing down by this time. The ends of the fingers were pale and wrinkled. All at once, after I had reached far back and yanked a great chunk of sod loose, the pressure on my right foot lessened, I pulled forward until I grunted, and the foot slowly came free.

In a moment I was on my knees, in another moment on my feet. Then, to my utter amazement, I was shaken by the most violent and uncontrollable chill I had ever experienced. My lower jaw shook, my whole frame shook. I could not take a sure step in any direction. I could hardly stand. Stumbling across the stream, I sprawled in a muddy spot for a while, moved forward on hands and knees, finally reached a sunny slope close to a little sod house. I could not stop shivering. I began to wonder whether I'd be able to walk at all.

After a long rest I limped across the garden plots to the

highway. Both legs were numb and undependable, but neither pained much. Slowly, by degrees, the shivering stopped. Slowly, step by step, I got back to Birkimelur, to my room on the third floor.

There the stately Sigrídur Einarsdóttir, not needing to be told that something had happened, said that if I soused the mud off my clothes in the bathtub she would take them to the basement to dry. She was concerned, but not fussy, and for this I was grateful. I told her that no bones had been broken. She seemed not to notice the blood on my face and hair. I soaked a while in the bathtub, put on fresh clothes, and went down to see the Pettingills.

"Now don't be alarmed," I said. "I'm all right, but I've had a remarkable experience." I could see by the looks on the two faces that my friends were more than bewildered. Eleanor's first thought was that there had been a real brawl this time at the coffee place I'd been telling them about.

VII

Independence Day in Reykjavík

FOR THREE DAYS one idea dominated all others: I must somehow keep up with the Pettingills. Getting into and out of bed was painful, but worst of all was pulling on and taking off socks and shoes. I thanked heaven I was able to manage by myself. The sudden stabs of pain were excruciating. I couldn't forego an occasional gasp or groan. My decisions about the accident were sensible. I knew no bones were broken. What I needed was not medicine, not taping or bandaging, but walking, walking of all sorts, activity of any kind involving legs, feet, and back.

There were, I confess, spells of morbid introspection. What if I had lain there all night, all the following day: who, eventually, would have found me? I imagined the sudden cry of the children, listening to their teacher there among the garden plots, standing on the ditch and seeing the half-buried corpse below them. I imagined the agony of the Pettingills, faced with the problem of informing my relatives yet of going ahead with their summer's work.

That first day I slept very late. No one said a word about my having been careless. Everyone expressed concern, but no one gave me the feeling that I'd become a problem. I did not feel up to field work, but I had a real desire to go to the old cemetery, to drink in the beauty of the flowers there, to walk by myself as slowly as I wished along the neat paths, to spell out and pronounce the wonderful names on the stones. Some of the dates had, I recalled, gone back a long, long way. Especially did I want to return to the fine monument honoring Pierre Loti, to reread the quotations in French from his *Iceland Fisherman*.

I took my drawing board along, and, thinking that I might eventually do a portrait of an adult redwing, I worked for some time on a section of birch branch on which I might put the bird. It was my intention to show some sky at the top, but the principal color of the background was to be the rich blue-gray of Esja, the majestic mountain off to the northeast. I sketched in the redwing, life-size, but never painted in any part of the picture.

It was Sunday. The people who visited the cemetery interested me deeply. Most of them seemed to be middle-aged. One fine-looking man strolled about for a long time, nodding each time he passed me, but evincing no interest in what I was drawing. The women wore long black dresses. The two long braids that hung down their backs were ribboned together at the very end. Their hats, which were without ornament, were small, flat caps. They wore a touch of gold—jewelry or trimming of some sort. What I noticed particularly was their bearing, the beauty of their faces. I longed to know them, to hear them tell of the homeland or sing the homeland's songs. The black dresses were obviously a costume of long standing. Most women in the shopping district had, I recalled, worn stylish clothes of the sort I'd seen in America, but some older women had worn this stately attire even there. I was much impressed by its austerity, its dignity, its authenticity.

Árni Waag wanted to show us a whimbrel nest he had found several kilometers south of the city. I was eager to observe the breeding behavior of this species, so decided to go along. The ride in the panel truck was comfortable enough, but the minute I set foot on the ground I knew I was not up to much of a walk. A pair of redshanks were scolding noisily near the road. Urging my friends to proceed without me, I stayed with the truck, thinking I might find a redshank chick. The redshanks did not trust me. I watched them a while as I stood near the road, then hobbled to a big chunk of lava, sat down with my back against it, and went sound asleep.

On the second day after the accident I felt much better. The Pettingills decided to take a two-hour drive to the farm of a famous birdbander, Hákon Vilhjálmsson, over near Keflavík. This man had found the nest of a gray (red) phalarope, a species which rarely nests in Iceland. After my friends had departed, I went to the cemetery, found a baby redwing barely out of the nest, and made a direct-from-life drawing of it. The simple little portrait turned out well.

After lunch, I walked down to the meadows. The wagtail brood had left the nest. When I looked at the mass of earth that had fallen, I marveled that I had been able to dig myself out. The redshank flew up from its nest when I was a

Independence Day in Reykjavík / 39

hundred yards away. The meadow pipit was so intent on incubating that she almost let me touch her. The snipe nest still held three eggs. Along the main ditch I came suddenly upon a hen mallard and three chicks. The behavior of that mother bird convinced me that she and I had met before. Not content with quacking loudly and scurrying off with her brood, she hissed and came at me. The three ducklings acted as if they didn't know what to make of their mother. As they looked about wildly, not knowing whether to go or wait, their cheeping seemed to say, "Mother, quit fooling with that man! Come back and take care of *us!*"

Independence Day there in Reykjavík I shall never forget, never as long as I live. I couldn't understand a word of the speeches and songs. No one paid any particular attention to the Pettingills and me as we strolled about, they with their cameras, I with my unsightly scars. The hundreds of flags and flowers made Austurvöllur, the big square in front of Parliament House, exceedingly bright. Flags of every nation seemed to be everywhere, yet not for the life of me could I find my own Stars and Stripes. I didn't say so to the Pettingills, but this hurt. I had taken a very small part in two wars. I wanted to salute something on anybody's Independence Day.

The reason I felt that way went very deep. I didn't care a hoot whether all these fine people knew that I was an American or whether they considered me patriotic. What I felt was that they themselves were truly patriotic; that they loved their country in the way a country should be loved; that I loved America just that way. There were no firecrackers. There was neither drinking nor make-believe. The thousands of people moved about in a dignified way, every one of them well dressed, every one of them proud. There must have been gumchewing and crackerjack-munching somewhere in Reykjavík on that seventeenth of June, 1958, but I certainly did not see it. The great throng stood as they listened to an hour or more of songs sung by good singers. Applause was enthusiastic and genuine, but it did not include whooping, yelling, and whistling. The people liked what they heard. They were made the happier and the more proud by it.

When the musical program was over, a whole section of Laekjargata became suddenly rhythmical as the dancing started. How joyful everyone seemed to be! As I passed my coffee place, I looked in through the windows, half-hoping that someone would wave at me, for I'd become something of an habitué there. But no one waved. With my dark suit on, instead of the red and black-checked woolen shirt I usually wore, I probably wasn't recognizable anyway.

One more bit of Independence Day was important. That morning, at the end of my round of nests in the meadows, I found a baby snipe. It was a long way from the nest I had been watching, which still held three eggs. It was a lovely, furry little thing, with a pattern of rich brown, buff, black, and silvery gray so intricate that after a half-hour of drawing I had to stand up, wave my arms, and stretch in sheer desperation. Part of the trouble was, of course, that the snipeling would not stand still. It was all over the place—in the middle of the paintbox one minute, under the couch or in a closet the next. It ran ever so nimbly, and, having no instinct with regard to tables, it ran off the top and dropped to the floor repeatedly. The tumbles did not seem to hurt it in the least.

Independence Day in Reykjavík / 41

VIII

From Reykjavík to Blönduós:
A Breath-Taking Trip

DEPARTURE FOR MÝVATN on June 18 was a flurry of conferences with the tall, powerful, blond Finnur Gudmundsson, who obviously was eager to make my stay as pleasant and profitable as possible, and who arranged for my permit to collect birds; of accompanying Gudrún Thorbergsdóttir from office to office while she obtained a driver's license for me; of selecting and packing that which would be needed for a stretch of work away from Reykjavík. Eleanor Pettingill did all the purchasing of food. Sewall was busy with photographic equipment. I decided against borrowing a shotgun, for I knew that I would get more painting done if I did no shooting.

Somewhere I had read that the traveler in Iceland was never out of sight of a glacier. As we drove eastward out of the city, then northward toward the deep, narrow inlet known as Hvalfjördur, I wondered which of the distant whitecaps and domes were glaciers and which were not, but the problem did not beset me in the least, for the whole broad vista was all so wonderful. The smoothness and greenness of the gentle, upswinging slopes thrilled me. Close to the dusty highway, mile after mile, ran the cement conduit for part of Reykjavík's hot water supply. Here and there we passed big, noble-looking houses of the farmsteads that had been established almost a thousand years before. A small, neat sign informed us that the highway leading right would take us to Thingvellir, where the Althing, the legislature, had been established in the year 930. Ahead and to the right rose dark Esja, now virtually free of snow, massive, sublime. At its foot we stopped to scan the heights above us with our binoculars and there, so tiny that they looked like bits of light-struck dust floating against the darkness of the pinnacles, were fulmar petrels, birds of the sea. This was one of their nesting places.

Hvalfjördur has never, so far as I know, been called the longest, mightiest, or most spectacular fjord in the world, but I feel sure that it must be one of these, if not all three. In going around it, we traveled for hours. The road was dusty and narrow. There were long one-way stretches, so that the driver was obliged to keep sharp lookout for the little orange markers at which it was possible to pull off while the other car passed. Traffic was not heavy, but there was no telling when a bright spurt of dust ahead might evoke from one of us a shout of "Car," "Truck," or "Bus," this to tell our driver that we had seen something coming. I never ceased to marvel at the speed of the trucks and busses which passed us. "It's all in the day's work," the roar and scattering of gravel seemed to affirm.

From Reykjavík to Blönduós / 43

We filled up with gas at the head of the fjord, then, having passed a whaling station in the course of an hour or so more of driving, returned to the outer coast not far from the village of Akranes. Everything across the water to our left seemed oddly familiar—the long slopes, the sky line, in particular a corkscrew-shaped mass of snow filling a high gully. With a peculiar sensation we realized that the road we could see so clearly just across the mouth of the fjord was the very one we had followed hours before. Oh, Iceland, thou givest thy visitors ample time for savoring the wild beauty of Hvalfjördur!

The word *beauty* calls to mind, paradoxically enough, the sheep that seemed to be part of every slope, every patch of green, every turn of the highway. We never saw many of them in any one place, but like the glaciers they were always in sight. Most of them were white, but some were black. Occasionally we saw a white ewe with two black lambs. What we continued to note, and unfailingly to laugh at, was the endless variation in the shapes of the ewe-mothers. Now that summer had arrived, their shaggy winter coats were dropping off. Their slender heads and necks were very short-haired, and these stuck out in such a way as to suggest that the naked animals had hastily thrown thick fleeces over themselves without bothering to check whether these were all in one piece. The wool was dirty underneath and behind, not so very clean looking anywhere, and exceedingly ragged. Some animals trailed literally yards of wool behind them, and this tangled in the shrubbery and blew in the wind. The ewes' pale eyes and steady gaze gave them a fearsome appearance, especially when they stamped a front foot. No steep was beyond their scaling. Lush grass grew at the very tops of the high talus slopes, and thither they were wont to go, taking their lambkins with them.

Much of the country was so very wild, so utterly without houses, fences, or other evidence of civilization that when we came to a crossroads, examined the neat signposts, and started off again, we wondered whether we could possibly be going in the right direction. The absence of billboards was a constant delight, but so used were we Americans to being told that Buck's Barby Cue was three miles ahead, or that Buzz Inn was around the next curve, that the dearth of signs was almost awesome.

Near the fine hostelry named Fornihvammur a swift stream came tumbling down from the high country to the north. The water was exceedingly clear and cold. In certain deep places, close to the rocky banks, little companies of harlequin ducks were gathered. Most of them appeared to be drakes. Their colors matched those of their surroundings so perfectly that they were hard to see. Their purplish-gray, black, and chestnut matched dark reflections of the mountains and sky, and their neat white spots, bars, and crescents matched bits of floating foam. Most of the time the birds headed upstream, keeping low in the water and close to the bank, but occasionally they whirled about, allowing themselves to be carried with the current until, arrived at another beloved nook or eddy, they began fighting the stream once more.

North of Fornihvammur the winding road climbed steadily. Often we crossed or drove alongside the Nordurá, the swift little river whose many tributaries rushed down from snowbanks not far from the highway. Breathtaking in their chaste beauty were two whooper swans flying downstream about a hundred feet in the air. How their gleaming whiteness contrasted with the dark gray of the mountains behind them! A raven flew out from a cliff, flapping along peacefully until a fierce little merlin attacked, forcing the big egg thief to twist, turn, side-slip, and roll over midair in its clumsy determination to get away unscathed.

We were in high, gray, barren country now, country to which summer had not yet come. We looked backward upon the green lowlands from which we had risen, then ahead across a lake-dotted plateau. The stream ended suddenly in a lake on which floated two red-throated loons. Snow lay in great patches about us, not on slopes above us this time. There were no such slopes now. Raw wind from the north drove wet snow against the windshield. This was Iceland of a sort we had not seen.

The snow flurry did not last long, and the wind, surprisingly enough, died down within an hour or so. We had supper in a clean, lovely spot near a neat bridge and pretty stream. To the east and south rose bold, snow-free mountains which looked as if they had been covered with greenish-gray felt. Eleanor performed wizardry in her kitchen in the panel truck. As we ate we were regaled by the mellow *tooleeoo* of golden plovers, the windy, trembling calls of the whimbrels, and the hooting of snipes—not to forget a meadow pipit whose flight songs were almost directly overhead. A great black-backed gull that flew toward us from the northwest changed course abruptly when attacked by a pair of whimbrels. The whimbrels, determined to drive this hated creature out of their nest territory, pummeled it thoroughly, hitting it broadside again and again. When we last saw the gull, it was twisting and turning frantically. Free at last of the first two whimbrels, it was now being beleaguered by another pair.

It was past ten o'clock when we came again within sight of the sea, and this time the pale gray-blue water stretched off grandly to the northward. The road led for a time along the edge of the bluff, and there the ocean lay, below us. Off to the northwest several hundred miles was Greenland, but directly to the north, between us and the vast polar mediterranean, there was no land. How I longed for a glimpse—just a glimpse—of a white-tailed eagle, the majestic bird the Icelanders called the *örn*. Presently we were in the village of Blönduós. After talking a while with the proprietor of the neat little inn, we went to bed.

IX

We See the Fálki

THE DRIVE FROM Blönduós to Akureyri took us through high country. The weather was pleasant enough as we ate breakfast beside the road at sea level, but as we climbed the mountains, we found ourselves first in misty clouds, then in cold, steady rain. The road, nowhere muddy, always narrow, often tortuous, climbed steadily. Below us, way off down the steep slopes, dark-blue and white little rivers rushed through narrow canyons. Never was our course straight; now we rounded the head of a narrow valley, now the shoulder of a broad slope, always climbing. It would have been interesting to stop, to listen for the roar of distant waterfalls, but nowhere was there a wide, safe-looking shoulder, nowhere a flat stretch of turf, and, furthermore, the unfamiliarity and austerity of our surroundings did not encourage loitering. This was no sightseeing trip. What sights we saw we had to see. There were no birds. Photography was out of the question. The thing to do was keep moving. Finally we reached the pass. All at once, without benefit of elevation marker or signboard, we realized that we were no longer climbing.

We knew we were headed east, but clouds obscured the slopes ahead of us. There was no horizon. The downgrade of the highway was not alarmingly steep, but proceeding in second gear seemed advisable much of the time, since the rain continued. How wild, how utterly wild this country was! Nowhere an intersection, nowhere a road leading off to one side, nowhere a house or store or filling station—yet always the neat, well-made highway, invariably sure of itself, unfailingly dependable, to remind us that all this wildness had been harnessed long ago. I could not help wondering when the road had been built, whether it followed some ancient trail, whether it could possibly be used all winter.

I was driving. Suddenly, downslope ahead, perhaps a hundred yards away, loomed an apparition that took my breath. Whatever it was, it was in the middle of the road, dead ahead. Successfully enough—that is to say, without throwing us off the road or turning us over—I applied the brakes. The apparition was moving toward us. It was a huge grader! Off to the right was a mist-hung chasm that looked bottomless. To the left, miracle of miracles, was a spot that might have been prepared for just such an exigency—a naked scraping or widening of the road. Onto this I drove with heart pounding, wondering whether we would slither into the ditch. We were a tense, wordless threesome. The grader toiled past us. "All in the day's work, my hearties! All in the day's work!" it seemed to roar.

There was a hint of break in the weather. Bright spots appeared in the gray sky. The rain slackened, stopped. We were losing elevation rapidly now, entering once more the green of lower slopes. We had picked up another stream, and this we followed faithfully through narrowings of the valley, across lush little meadows, downward, ever downward. As clouds to the north lifted, the lower slopes of black mountains came sharply into view. There were patches of snow at all levels, and so similar in tone was the white of the snow to that of the sky that wherever the snow was continuous across the front of a mountain, all the rock above it seemed to be suspended. The illusion was astounding, almost frightening.

Patches of blue sky opened up. The clouds so withdrew from one remarkable mountain that at last we saw it in all its majesty. It was not by any means the largest peak of the area. It may not have been especially high, but its top third was narrowly pointed, and as I looked at those far crags, about which wisps of cloud still lingered, I was powerfully exhilarated. I wanted to climb them, to look down from them toward the sea. Remembering how Árni Waag, back at Reykjavík, had never failed to give me the name of every mountain, lake, or peninsula I asked about, I was sorry he was not with us. He would know the name of this jagged peak, and the name itself would be beautiful.

Akureyri, the second largest city of Iceland, we found to be neat, brightly painted, and lively. Most of the buildings were of cement. For several miles they stretched along the shore, not pinched in between cliffs and high-tide marks as I'd expected they would be, but comfortably spread over the gentle slope not far back from the water's edge.

In our approach from the west, we had not had much of a look at the city, but as we climbed the huge mountain to the east, we saw the whole of it well. Crossing this mountain involved negotiating two sets of hairpin curves, one set on the way up, one on the way down. On one of the curves, on the way up, I found that the second gear was not powerful enough to take us forward, so, shifting to what I supposed to be low, I was dumfounded, horrified, to realize that we were moving backward. I stepped hard on the foot brake and we came to a dead stop. Traffic was not heavy. No blast of horn, either behind or ahead, announced to the world my incompetency. There we stood, the driver, exasperated, howsoever unjustly, with the machine age rather than with himself, until the proper gear had been engaged and all brakes released, when off we roared, unscathed, upward.

As we began the descent we perceived that the great valley below us was different from any we had seen in Iceland. At the bottom was a fine large river, the Fnjóská, whose course was fairly straight. The whole vista, aside from the sky, was a study in green—the familiar bright green of grass, with its irregular dotting of sheep, the pale grayish-green of lichen, and the rich dark green of birch trees. The birches grew in straggly patches on the higher slopes, but along the river and for considerable distances upslope on either side they were a continuous mass. This was the far-famed Vaglaskógur, a woodland of which the people were very proud. We recalled hearing that when the vikings had come to Iceland in early times, they had found extensive stands of low birch woods or birch "scrub" in the valleys and lowlands, but the trees had not been large enough to furnish lumber for boats, houses, and furniture. The great birch forest was under rigid governmental supervision now. Most of the trees appeared to be about fifteen to twenty feet high, but many were higher.

The bridge across the river was so delicate in appearance that I felt touches of cold fear as we approached. Considerably higher in the middle than at either end, it was well designed and well built. Great busses had been traveling over it for years. But so narrow was it that one felt almost duty bound to stop before entering, to measure both car and bridge.

As we were driving through high, open country between this bridge and the big waterfall known as Godafoss (pronounced "Gód-tha-foss"), we had an unexpected thrill when a gyrfalcon appeared out of nowhere, flew so close that we could see the barring on its wings, back, and tail, and alighted on a low rock not far from the highway. Sewall, who was at the wheel, saw it first. "God, it's a gyrfalcon!" he said in a hushed, tense voice, and from the screeching of brakes and rattling of equipment I knew he had photography in mind. I never saw him so beside himself with excitement. Cameras and tripods were yanked out as if they'd been garden tools. Eleanor had a telephoto lens ready for him in a twinkling. As for me, I had my glass on the bird and I looked hard. The gyrfalcon sat there with wings loosely folded, looking calmly, regally, off in the direction in which it had been headed, then toward us. Its perch was not dramatic in the least. The whole area was flat. The scene was not in any way "composed"; there was nothing balanced about its few simple elements. But so beautiful was that single bird as it stood there, so majestic and powerful, that it needed no special lighting to give it appeal, no background of crag to make one hungry for a further look. There came to mind the image of Pierre Loti's magnificent fisherman, Yann Moan, described as "of those men whom anything becomes." Assuredly the words seemed to fit this gyrfalcon, this *fálki* of the Icelanders. Put the bird anywhere and its very perch became magnificent. Sewall had his movie camera half set up when the *fálki* sprang easily into the air and, beating its wings rapidly, made off northeastward not far above ground.

Godafoss, the waterfall just mentioned, was only a short way upriver from a big bridge on the highway. A side road took us to a point from which we could see mist rising and hear the heavy roar. The country here was rough. Between us and the river were dips, ridges, heaps of great rocks, a sheltered spot covered thickly with knee-high birches. Wherever we looked there were moss and lichens, but beneath this soft covering was lava. Of the many flowers, I noticed in particular the little white dryas or avens, a plant I had seen so often in the American Arctic. Many of the ground-hugging shrubs were in blossom, but I looked in vain for anything resembling what English-speaking people in Ungava and on the Labrador called the "bake-apple." Part of the time the sun was out, but nowhere did we see a butterfly.

As for birds, our first impression was that there weren't any; but presently we were hearing the whistles of a golden plover standing guard on a little eminence not far away, the bubbling calls of whimbrels in the distance, and the bright song of a snow bunting off toward the river.

My limp continued to be bothersome, so rather than hurrying to the fall, I contented myself with what I could find near the road. A narrow straggling stand of birch on the sheltered side of a lava fold attracted my attention. It would be hard to explain why, as I walked toward these birches, I began thinking about a ptarmigan nest. We had not yet seen or heard a ptarmigan. I don't recall having seen either feathers or droppings in the vicinity, but as I walked along the lower edge of the birch patch I kept thinking, over and over, that if I were a ptarmigan I'd choose this sort of place for a nest. I recall standing in a certain spot and looking across and down at the interlaced birch branches perhaps ten feet away. I recall sensing that something bright had drawn my eye back for a second look, and there, her lovely plumage filling the shallow bowl of her nest just to the brim, was a hen rock ptarmigan. Often I had been startled by unexpectedly seeing a bird close to me, but this time I had been thinking ptarmigan so hard and long that the discovery didn't quite surprise me. The thrill was real enough, but it was complex: not only had I found the nest; I had justified completely my belief that it was there. My voice must have had a strong note of egotism in it as I announced the discovery to the Pettingills.

Sewall took photographs before we tried getting closer to the bird. Then I crept toward her with hand outstretched, hoping to touch or stroke her. When the tips of my fingers were within inches of her, the hen fluttered off a few feet, stretched her neck up full length, and flicked her tail. The eleven eggs were brown, heavily speckled with black.

Now began a long session of photography wherein I, directed by Sewall, drove the hen about rapidly enough to keep action vivacious, slowly enough to preserve the confiding expression of our heroine's face. Oh, she was a beauty! Her form was trim, her coloration elegant, her every step graceful. Now I was to coax her up a little acclivity if possible, now down toward some flowers which would add a pleasing color note. I continued to wonder where the cock was. Later we found him, perhaps a hundred yards away. Not yet having molted his winter plumage, he was dirty white. The hen, so far as we could tell, had finished the molt into her dark summer plumage.

The sun was so bright that Sewall had a time of it deciding what to photograph first. Eleanor reported a golden plover which had flopped along in the moss ahead of her, feigning injury. After a painstaking search we found the nest (four eggs) among rocks high on the slope of a gully, in the bottom of which lay wet snow three feet thick. Not far from the plover nest we saw a snow bunting enter a hole in the lava. We were sure it had a nest there, but neither shouting nor striking the lava repeatedly with a rock induced it to fly out.

When, at length, we went to the river for a picnic lunch, we were surprised at the depth of the canyon through which the water churned and boiled. In the vertical rock wall directly across from us were symmetrical shapes that looked vaguely like a row of gigantic fossil ferns, tips downward. These were, I guessed, cross sections of lava streams.

On examining the map, we found that we were still a long way from Mývatn. As we resumed our journey, the thoughts uppermost in my mind were that we were leaving those precious ptarmigan and golden plover eggs behind us; that driving back for chicks to paint would be arduous and time consuming; and that, worst of all, there was no telling when the chicks would arrive. These misgivings were justified. During my entire stay in Iceland I found only one ptarmigan chick, and not until the eve of my departure did I obtain a baby golden plover.

On a lake off to the north, below highway level, we spied two large dark birds low in the water well out from shore.

We See the Fálki / 55

They were great northern divers or common loons. Finnur Gudmundsson had told us that this species was of special interest to all British ornithologists who visited Iceland.

Off in the distance to the east we could now see the gleam of a vast, island-dotted sheet of water in which there was not the slightest reflection of the high mountains beyond. Mývatn at last! Presently we were looking down on, then driving alongside, the swift river that flowed out of the great lake's southwestern corner. All along this river harlequin ducks were common. The handsome birds were sunning themselves on the banks, swimming in deep eddies close to shore, flying upstream and down. The flying birds invariably kept above water and stayed low—low enough to pass under the very lowest of the bridges. The river was the Laxá, a cold stream, famous for its salmon.

The highway led eastward to the south of Mývatn, following the shore line part of the time, occasionally crossing a brook but never an arm of the lake. Low hills sometimes hid the main body of water from sight. Much of the land to the south of the highway was flat and marshy, but nowhere did we see a stand of sedge or rush extensive enough to provide a habitat for water rails. This species was, we had been told, rare and nonmigratory in Iceland.

Along the east side of the lake we passed through a veritable wonderland of lava chimneys, spires, towers, arches and causeways, many of them standing in, and perfectly reflected by, motionless water. This was worth traveling across the world to see. Never had I imagined anything like it! Nestled in sheltered places among the grotesqueries were more birch trees, some of them the largest we had seen, with trunks up to almost a foot in diameter at the base. The leaves were not fully out. Summer had not yet arrived in this north-eastern part of Iceland.

Along the edge of a lava bed not far from the lake shore, a rough-and-tumble area throughout which the roots of the birches went down into the very rock, we saw two more cock ptarmigan, both of them in soiled white winter feather. They were standing about thirty feet apart. As they flew off they cackled loudly enough to be heard above the noise made by the truck.

We reached our neat little hotel, Reynihlíd, not too late for supper of sweet, pink berry soup, something wholly new to our experience, tomatoes and cucumbers, and delicious cold smoked mutton. On another table in the dining doom stood a bowl full of boiled wild duck eggs, still in the shell. I still do not know what kept me from walking off with some of these.

The date was June 19. There would be daylight around the clock. Before turning in for the night, we drove back to a stretch of shore that had caught our eye. There we identified several species of ducks, found a scaup's nest containing four pale olive-gray eggs in a tuft of grass at the water's edge, and received our initiation by the midges. The lake had, we decided, been well named, for the midges were everywhere. They were dipterans of the family Chironomidae. They buzzed about our ears and eyes and crawled under our clothing hundreds at a time, but they did not bite. The flies that did bite occasionally were black flies of the family Simuliidae, bloodthirsty pests remembered all too vividly by Sewall and me, for together we had endured week after week of them at Churchill, Manitoba, in the summer of 1931. The larvae of the midges lived in quiet water but the larval simuliids required swiftly running water like that of the Laxá. Whenever the midges were especially bad we found solace in realization that there was not a mosquito in Iceland.

A pleasant surprise, back at the hotel, was a visit from Michael and Georgiana Savage, a lively young English couple who were catching harlequin ducks for Peter Scott's collection of living waterfowl at Slimbridge. We had seen the Savages' white tents off to the left of the highway as we had started downslope for the Laxá. Already they had caught some birds, but they were trying for more. They had caught them in big nets hung from bridges. So wed to the water were the birds that they refused to fly anywhere except a very few feet directly above it, so into the nets they had flown, sometimes several of them at once. They were to be sent to England by air, as promptly as possible, from Akureyri.

I was bold enough to ask the Savages if they could let me have one of their birds for a direct-from-life portrait. They offered to take me right back to the Laxá, to let me participate in the whole netting operation, but I didn't feel up to limping around any more that day. They promised to catch a harlequin for me if they could.

X

Investigating Mývatn

WE PLANNED to sleep at Reynihlíd during our stay at Mývatn but to eat our meals in the panel truck wherever our work chanced to take us. Food we would obtain at the hotel kitchen—beautiful big trout fresh from the lake, slabs of smoked mutton, bread, cheese, butter, cucumbers, tomatoes, and cookies. We had with us some excellent packaged soup which Eleanor had bought in Reykjavík.

I wakened early enough on June 20 to have a real look at our surroundings—the bold mountain to the northeast, now almost free of snow; the curiously furrowed masses of lava that sprawled over a vast area from the lake's shore northward; the little church, with its belfry and cross, its white picket fence, and its garden of bright flowers; and the old houses, partly of wood, partly of sod, that stood in a solid row across the road from the hotel. Small peninsulas along the lake shore seemed to be inhabited by arctic terns and black-headed gulls, and I judged from the incessant bickering that the two species were nesting side by side. I could hear whimbrels and golden plovers calling from the high country to the east.

We breakfasted at six o'clock about a mile south of the hotel at the edge of the rough-and-tumble lava area through which the one and only road led. The place was fascinating. Fine birches grew wherever there was lava, but not on the smooth grassy slopes. The huge, oddly shaped rocks were piled on each other in haphazard fashion and we were careful as we walked amongst them lest we jar them loose. Under and between them were openings of all sorts, some cavernous and deep. Moss, lichens, and shrubbery blurred and softened the sharp edges. To the sides of the holes, way down in the semidarkness, clung delicate ferns. Where soil had accumulated, a thin mat of grass and avens grew, not to mention other pretty flowering plants whose names I did not know. Delightful it was to hear, and instantly to recognize, the bright tinkling song of a wren, the species known as the winter wren in America. Finnur Gudmundsson had told us that the wren was not common in Iceland, so we rejoiced at finding it. On a rough eminence not far from the lake shore, Sewall found a gadwall's nest containing seven buff-colored eggs. After watching a wheatear for some time, we saw it enter a hole under a rock, but we could not reach the nest. White wagtails seemed to be everywhere. Busy catching flies, they flew with beakfuls of these back into the shadowy recesses, but we found neither nest nor chick. Out on the lake we saw, in addition to species already mentioned, pintails, mallards, teal, and Slavonian grebes. Arctic terns dived at us fiercely whenever we went to inspect the gadwall's nest, so we felt sure that there were tern eggs or chicks close by.

On our way to the Savages' camp we proceeded in leisurely fashion along the south side of the lake, observing birds as we went. The midges were bad, so bad indeed that I wished I had brought a head net with me. At certain marshy spots dunlins were nesting in considerable numbers. Occasionally we saw widgeons, a handsome species that I did not know at all well. At one stop we watched a golden plover performing a wonderful courtship flight, soaring slowly two hundred feet or so above dry ground, pouring forth plaintive long-drawn-out whistles. On a narrow, grassy peninsula we found several scaup nests with obviously incomplete sets of eggs, an oldsquaw nest with four eggs (the down was very dark), and, well away from all these, under a bank within a few feet of the water's edge, a tufted duck's nest. This species I had seen only once before, in the spring of 1938, in the vicinity of Rouen, France.

No one was stirring at the Savages' camp when we got there. We did not want to disturb them, for they might, for all we knew, have been up all night catching harlequins. We decided to see what we could of the Laxá. I observed along the river that morning more harlequins than I had seen since my visit to the Straits of Georgia, off the east coast of Vancouver Island, in 1934, and since my period of temporary duty on Attu, at the western end of the Aleutian chain, in the early spring of 1944. So close to the water did the birds stay at all times that even those which climbed out for a bit of sunning or preening kept one toe in, so to speak. Learning from observation which spots they liked best, I crawled up for a look at them through the tall grass. Surprised, they did not fly, but dived instead, and never could

I tell which direction they were taking or where they were likely to reappear. Since I continued to see far more drakes than hens I felt sure that many hens were on nests. The Savages had told us of a nest with six eggs that a farmer had shown them.

While I was watching the harlequins, a pair of graylag geese flew over, the first I had ever seen in the wild. Their honking was gentle, almost conversational, their flight slow and easy. I had no idea where their nest might be.

The Savages had a fine hen harlequin for me, and this we took with us in a big cardboard box. Some drakes and hens that they had caught were to be sent to England that day. I did not envy the Savages the long drive to Akureyri nor the harlequins their flight away from this lovely nesting ground.

Back at Reynihlíd I set to work. My model was amazingly agile and strong. I let her crawl through the sleeve of a heavy shirt and pinned her there fast, with head out; even so, she often kicked and struggled until she toppled to one side, sleeve and all. The bird could not have been in pain, but certainly she was uncomfortable and probably she was badly frightened. As I think back on the experience, I wonder whether the end attained wholly justified the means. This I know about my drawing: it was far more lifelike than it could possibly have been had I worked solely with a dead specimen.

Since the sun was bright and the air warm most of the day, the Pettingills, busy with their photography, suffered badly from the midges. Wearing the head nets was disagreeable, to say the least, but the impossibility of clearing the

Day-old redshank chick caught and painted direct from life
June 24, 1958, along the east side of Mývatn,
northeastern Iceland.

MÁRÍATLA

Young white wagtail just after leaving the nest.
Painted direct from life at Mývatn,
northeastern Iceland, June 28, 1958.

lenses of midges, of taking good photographs on a day when light conditions were excellent—this was heartbreaking.

Toward evening a north breeze sprang up, the air turned cold, and almost immediately the flies disappeared. The sky turned deep gray, almost black, but the lake's brightness was like that of burnished silver. Fog gathered about the dark headlands and islets, slowly obscuring them. Long scarves of white hid the bases of the distant mountains, then the far shore, then vast stretches of the gleaming water. Even as we wondered whether all this was beautiful, or whether "eerie" might be a better word for it, Mývatn disappeared.

XI

A Search in Vain

On SATURDAY, JUNE 21, the Pettingills and I covered afoot some beautiful rough country northeast of Mývatn in hopes of finding gyrfalcons. We had long known that these great birds of prey were uncommon in Iceland. Our friend Finnur had forewarned us that we might not see many of them, for their numbers had fluctuated with those of their favorite prey species, the ptarmigan, and ptarmigan were now rare. The gyrfalcon had received strict governmental protection since 1940. No one, not even an official of the Museum of Natural History, could now obtain a permit to collect a gyrfalcon or its eggs. Scattered pairs were known to breed in certain wild areas. Mývatn was one of these areas. I had never, in all my wanderings through the American north country, found a gyrfalcon's nest, and Sewall quite naturally felt that if his film was to represent Icelandic bird life at all properly, it should contain some good gyrfalcon footage. The gyrfalcon was Iceland's national bird.

Finnur had advised us to learn from a man named Sverrir Tryggvason just where the Mývatn gyrfalcons lived. We had found this competent, well-informed man without difficulty, for he lived just across the road from Reynihlíd and was building a new house only a hundred yards or so away. He had assured us that the gyrfalcon eyrie was close by, that we should have no difficulty in reaching it. We had tucked this bit of intelligence comfortably away, not inquiring about details since problems concerning other species had continued to present themselves.

After my long bout of harlequin painting, I felt a need for stretching my legs, so I went to Sverrir Tryggvason and talked with him about gyrfalcons for some time. He had visited the Mývatn eyrie early that spring; there had been eggs, not chicks, when he had last climbed to the nesting ledge. "The place is not very far from here—just the other side of the hill you see there," he said, pointing northward to a bald knob on whose top I could see a wind sock. I had not realized until that moment that there was any sort of landing field in the Mývatn area.

Now it has long been a habit of mine, on receiving directions as to how to reach a certain place, to memorize distances and relationships not as they actually are, but as I come, during the discussion, to envision them. Sverrir Tryggvason's statement conveyed the all-important, basic idea that the eyrie was not far away, that it was, indeed, just beyond the hill he had pointed out. This I reported, with conviction, to the Pettingills, so off we set after breakfast, wondering a little why, if the gyrfalcons were so near, we had

A Search in Vain / 65

not seen one, wondering also where, in the vicinity of this apparently smooth-sloped eminence, there could be a cliff high enough to attract gyrfalcons.

I hesitate to say how much of our lives we gave to this vain search. I clung stubbornly to my belief that the eyrie was really close by. I investigated every bit of rough slope, every perpendicular rock face, every dip, every rise, every likely looking spot within the square mile "the other side of the hill," and of course found nothing. The Pettingills also searched, and with determination, in another quarter. We decided that something was wrong. The possibility crossed my mind that Sverrir Tryggvason had pointed to a hill different from that to which I *thought* he had pointed.

So back we went to Reynihlíd, and this time we learned that, before even starting to walk, we should drive a mile farther north along the highway than we had. Then, bearing in mind that for a considerable stretch we would not be able to see the cliff itself, we should make our way northeastward from the highway—first past a square green field, then across a great stretch of lava, then past four lakes, then up across a sort of divide to higher country, then along a deep valley or canyon to the cliff itself. Sverrir Tryggvason's adjective for the cliff was "little," but by this time I had decided to make generous allowance for understatement. A proper gyrfalcon, especially an Iceland *fálki*, would require a sizable cliff, of that I was certain—some "little" cliff like those on Ailsa Craig or the notorious Eiger.

I recall with what resolve we left the truck, marched past the rectangular green field, and started across the rough stretch of lava for the nearest of the four lakes. Despite my limp, I kept up fairly well. Skirting the edge of the first lake involved a bit of wading. A pretty meadow bordered the second. The third was at the foot of a steep hill, whose shoulder we negotiated following a sheep trail. The fourth we passed in only a general way, and I am not sure to this day that we took the correct course when, after a last look in hope of seeing the truck, now miles away, we began the climb. Here there was no trail of any sort; but the configuration of the slopes was obvious enough. At the head of the valley there was no cliff worthy of a second glance. If there was a cliff of any sort anywhere in this area, it would have to be beyond the ridge to the north, in the next valley.

No longer were the three of us together. Sewall had his ideas about where the cliff was, Eleanor had hers, and I suppose I had mine, though I was somewhat at a loss after my firm beliefs of the morning had been so thoroughly shattered. So eager were we to see the gyrfalcons that we gave no thought to the possibility of sudden weather change. So determined were we to find the cliff that we had no time for enjoying the beauty that was now spread so lavishly behind and below us. I have a vague memory of the four gleaming lakes, of tiny dots on them that I knew to be grebes, of the distant Mývatn, calm and bright, of the mountains off to the south, topped with snow. Finally, with a scramble through birch scrub up a steepish stretch, I made the top of the ridge. Ahead and below was a narrow wild valley, almost a canyon, at the head of which, largely obscured by a secondary ridge or flank, was a cliff. A wonderful cliff it was, too, with strata that were bowed upward. Scrutinizing what I could see with the binocular, I discerned no whitewashing of the sort that is nearly always conspicuous below a falcon's eyrie. After a brisk walk along the top of the ridge, I joined the Pettingills, and together we had a careful look. From this vantage point we could see much more of the cliff. *Little* indeed! It was several hundred feet high.

Carrying cameras, tripods, and lenses this great distance without the aid of horses would be unthinkable. Disappointed, almost dejected, we started back for the highway. We had not by any means reached the base of the cliff. We had left the lovely place not knowing whether gyrfalcons were there or not. But I was downright glad when, an hour or so later, the three of us climbed into comfortable old "Big Blue" unscathed.

After a rest we set to work again. The Pettingills had found a snow bunting nest in the rocks about a mile south of Reynihlíd. Here, after taking such photographs as they needed, they caught a chick for me to paint. My model squatted comfortably in my left hand as I worked with my right. The sketch was only fair; I was not very well satisfied with it. The breeding of this species so close to the birch trees struck me as peculiar. In Arctic America I had found the snow bunting nesting only well north of the limit of trees, in piles of rubble or in deep cracks in the rocks. One nest had been in a hole under a window in a building at a Hudson's Bay Company trading post, another in an Eskimo grave.

Word had got round by this time that we three "birdmen" were in the neighborhood, so, not greatly to my surprise, I learned that two red-breasted mergansers and a Slavonian grebe had been brought in for me. These species the Icelanders called, respectively, the *toppönd* (or *litla toppönd*) and the *sefönd* or *flórgodi*. The birds had been caught in fish nets, many of which were now in constant use on the lake. The specimens were in a refrigerator across the road from the hotel. I climbed down a stout ladder into the subterranean shed, waited for my eyes to adjust to the semidarkness, and saw my three birds lying there on the ice and snow. They were still quite wet. The grebe's head I sketched after I had dried it out, and I prepared the specimen as a skin. It had lovely scarlet-pink irides, each pupil was encircled by a ring of creamy white, and there was a narrow line of reddish featherless skin which connected each eyelid with the base of the bill.

During our evening meal at what had become our regular eating place—a wide spot in the road a mile south of Reynihlíd—we had the briefest of looks at a gyrfalcon. The bird flew over rather high, but somehow its presence served to climax and validate our experiences of the morning.

Eleanor's principal ornithological contribution to the conversation was a lively account of a black-headed gull colony she had discovered among birch trees near a lake. The nests were on the ground, not in the trees. Nowhere had she found any chicks. The eggs had not yet hatched.

Early the following morning the Pettingills drove back to Godafoss. They needed more ptarmigan and golden plover pictures. I remained at the hotel, studied my captive snow bunting chick at length, and decided to draw it again. The second drawing was better in some ways than the first. I also tried a landscape showing the grebe, a drawing of the whole bird swimming, with a bit of reedy lake shore as the background, but the effort did not come off. My model was dead. There was something disproportionate about the layout.

Rather disgusted, and more convinced than ever that I could not do acceptable work without living models, I set out to study the grebes. I had looked at them from time to time, noticing that they were all in handsome breeding attire and that they were almost invariably in pairs. The species was not new to me. I had seen it repeatedly in various parts of North America. Nowhere about Mývatn had I seen what I would call a proper grebe nesting place. Nowhere had I seen a real stand of cattails or bulrushes. The birds were all about me and they seemed to be settled for the summer, but could they actually be nesting?

The question was answered directly enough as I walked along the grassy shore, noting a smooth furrow in the water —the sort of furrow a muskrat makes as it moves off just beneath the surface. I traced the furrow back to the oddest little excuse for a nest I had ever seen—a spot of mud about six inches in diameter, barely above water level, and lined with a wet wisp or two of weed, about a foot out from shore. In it was a longish, very pale blue, somewhat chalky-looking egg. By this time the grebe itself had come up several rods out in the lake. It and its mate were looking at me calmly enough; but the instant I raised my glass, under they both went so rapidly, so effortlessly, that I doubted my senses. I could touch the nest without the slightest trouble—no wading, no wet feet, just a simple reaching across with my hand from the solid shore. Never had I seen a grebe nest anything like this!

Before my observation of grebes was over, I had found two more nests, one of them as easily reachable from the shore as the first, the other a little farther out, in water perhaps a foot deep. In neither nest was there a full set of eggs. So completely exposed were the nests and so startlingly visible the eggs that I wondered how the species could hope to maintain itself.

My noon meal, which I carried in my pocket, I ate on a point of land that I had often viewed from afar but never visited. Here there was breeze enough to keep down the midges. As I sought a high spot from which I could look in several directions out over the lake, I came upon an amusing semidomestic scene—a mother sheep and her two lambs, all in a sort of cave, with their heads stuck into a crevice where, presumably, there were very few midges. On seeing me, the three animals bolted, of course. A few rods away the mother stopped, gave a peremptory bleat which halted the lambs, and they all gazed at me balefully with their grayish-yellow eyes.

That evening at the hotel the Pettingills told a tale of woe —of midges and light conditions so bad that photography had not been possible before midafternoon, of an empty ptarmigan nest about which lay the barred and mottled plumage of the beautiful hen, of a disconsolate-looking cock ptarmigan that seemed to be unable to leave the scene of the tragedy. Our guess was that a fox had killed and eaten the hen and eggs, but this was no more than a guess. The male ptarmigan was largely in winter plumage, but so worn and soiled were its feathers that it was pale gray rather than white. Why the molt into dark summer feather should proceed so much more rapidly in the hen than in her mate puzzled us. How, we continued to ask ourselves, could retention of a conspicuous white *male* plumage throughout the period of egg laying and incubation be advantageous to the ptarmigan in its struggle for survival? Granted that such a plumage might lead predators to capture the male rather than the female; granted that no predator would reason that where there is a male ptarmigan in early summer there might also be a female; granted that a hen ptarmigan could hatch and rear a brood without the help of a mate once the eggs had been laid; granted even that the species might survive despite the killing of every adult male during the period of incubation—granted all this, we continued to wonder why the spring molt of the male should not keep step with the advancing season along with the molt of the female.

The hotel was a madhouse after dinner. The noise of excited conversation, of hearty greeting, of stamping feet and banging doors continued all night long. Busloads of newcomers overran the place. Everybody was dressed in field garb and the hallways were piled high with sleeping bags and other gear. Some of the people were from England, we learned, but most of them were Icelanders here for a sip, a taste, a deep draught of their beloved Iceland. How I enjoyed their heartiness, their obvious exhilaration. They were here! Mývatn at last! The wilderness of northeastern Iceland lay all about them!

XII

Navels of Devils

MONDAY, JUNE 23, was cloudy and cool. I wakened very early
and, not knowing what time it was—my wrist watch had
stopped in the night—I listened in vain for rustlings in the
Pettingill room, got up and dressed, tiptoed down the hall
and across the little lobby, and let myself out the heavy front
door. Not knowing where, in this land of infinite possibilities,
I would be most likely to find a bird wholly new to me, I
decided to head northwestward straight into a vast, low-
lying bed of lava which had from the first attracted me. The
bed stretched for miles along the lake shore and back toward
the mountains. At a distance it appeared to be utterly barren, but when I entered it I soon perceived that lichens and
other small plants were growing there. Its monotony was austere, and I found that, despite my eagerness to discover what
lived in the lava itself, I tended to follow the shore, to pay
special attention to the clumps of grass there, to investigate

every depression in which vegetation was thick enough to hide the rock. I recalled that in Iceland some species of birds, the purple sandpiper for example, were alleged to nest only in the most desolate barrens. The purple sandpiper I had seen much of on Baffin and Southampton islands in the American Arctic. On Baffin, in the vicinity of Lake Amadjuak, I had been on its nesting grounds. Indeed, David F. Parmelee and I had obtained well-developed chicks there. But never had I found a nest or held a newly hatched chick in my hand.

Whether purple sandpipers have ever been found nesting in the lava near Mývatn I cannot say, but I saw two of them that morning well back from shore, running together up and down the rough rock on their shortish, orange-yellow legs. I am not sure that they were paired. They may have been of the same sex, and they did not act as if they were nesting. Put to flight, they moved swiftly off, not toward the lake but eastward into the high country.

Among grass within a few inches of the water I found several arctic tern nests and a recently hatched chick or two, one of which I took as a specimen. The parent birds attacked fiercely from behind, striking me hard on the head several times, and screaming *kee-arr, kee-arr* in a harsh voice. No black-headed gulls were nesting in this area, though I had seen them flying across it several times on their way to the little church, whose roof peak was a favorite resting place.

Failing to find a bird of any sort nesting in the lava back from the lake shore, I returned to Reynihlíd, found everyone blissfully asleep, tried the front door, which had locked itself in closing, and decided to head eastward, directly uphill. Three-quarters of the way to the top I had one of the surprises of my life—not a bird's nest, fox's den, or strange flower, but a miniature farmstead made by children in their play. Here were several little sod houses, a rectangular hay-field surrounded by a neat three-strand wire fence about five inches high, a carefully laid out road and plastic toy truck, even a cluster of graves, each with a tiny headstone. Had I been asked to list "attractions" which might be seen near Mývatn, I'm sure I'd never have listed any such item as this. I sat down near the sod houses, each of which was about as big as my shoe, and could not resist the thought that the young builders had derived a joy and satisfaction from work of this sort that they could not possibly have derived from watching television. Then, noting how far below me the hotel and other buildings were, I wondered whether I might not be the only adult in the world to have seen this remark-able playground.

On the bald heights above the miniature farm I came upon a pair of whimbrels and a loose flock of golden plovers. The plovers whistled as they flew up, but they did not go far, for this was a favorite feeding ground. The plump birds were not in pairs. They may have been paired, but they were go-ing about together in a flock. They moved deliberately this way and that in short runs, bowing stiffly and jabbing at the moss at the end of each run.

Back near the hotel once more, by this time fairly belliger-ent about breakfast, I saw a male wheatear fly with a mouth-ful of insects across the road directly in front of me. The bird must have been used to human beings, for promptly it popped into a hole in a low stone wall. I could not hear the chicks begging for food, so they must have been small. Soon the parent flew out with a large white fecal sac in its bill.

This it carried to the middle of the nearby pasture and dropped while flying. I tried to feel the nest, but it was beyond the reach of my fingers. The old birds gave an alarm note which sounded like *chack*. I had heard this note from the wheatears at the head of Frobisher Bay on Baffin Island hundreds of times.

After breakfast the Pettingills and I decided that we could no longer stay away from "the stacks"—those fantastic arches and pillars of lava that we had marveled at each time we had driven along the east side of the lake. This wonderland was obviously a park or estate of some sort, for a well-built road led into it, and there was a sturdy metal gate, painted green, and a neat sign, whose message we could not translate, at the entrance. Not far beyond the gate rose a bluff hill at whose north end stood jagged monoliths, each mirrored perfectly in the quiet water. There was water at the other side of the road also, but so completely hidden from view was the main body of Mývatn that we could not tell whether all this water belonged to one lake or to several.

The "stacks" side road led southward and westward along the base of the bluff hill, then steeply up around the hill's south end. Considerably to our surprise, we found the gate unlocked and easy to open. Leaving the truck outside the fence, and not without misgivings, we walked along the road. Soon we realized that many of the trees about us had been planted there—furry larches, healthy-looking small pines, graceful clumps of mountain ash or rowanberry. A plot of pansies near the road's steep climb was breathtakingly pretty. So abundant were the birds, and so wholly captivated were we by them, that we soon forgot all about the gate, fence, and sign. Within a surprisingly short time we had found a gadwall's nest with six eggs in the grass beneath a little birch, and a redwing's nest so far down in a hole among the rocks that we could hardly see the five eggs for the darkness. The outcry of the redwings reminded us that we were trespassing, but we were not to be deterred.

In a windless, grass-lined spot, a nook surrounded by birches and rocks as big as houses, a red-necked phalarope fluttered up with a sharp twitter a few feet in front of me, exposing to view four downy chicks, all in a huddle, each yellowish buff with dark markings. They could not have been more than a few hours old, yet off they scrambled in four directions. The parent bird was, I took care to observe, the male. Where the mother bird was, I had no way of knowing. I took one of the brood, for this was exactly the plumage stage I wanted to record in my direct-from-life painting.

Beyond a treeless stretch of lowland, all of it deeply carpeted with reindeer moss, I glimpsed more water, and again I could not be sure whether this was part of Mývatn. What I saw looked like a long, narrow pond. But for its having no current, I might have thought it a river. In a tangle of willows along a swampy bit of shore I stayed close to the water, for I did not want to miss any bird that might be swimming or wading there. I could not move forward without making considerable noise. Suddenly there was a loud scuttling sound, a splash, and harsh grunts as a hen red-breasted merganser scurried from the thicket and swam off, head held slim and high in agitation. Locating the nest was not easy, for it was well hidden among rocks and roots. There were eleven eggs. A well-defined path led from the nest to the water's edge.

Among the notable birds we saw that morning were four

female Barrow's goldeneyes, idling in the placid water. This was a duck I wanted very much to know better. Something told us that, despite our not having seen a drake, we were on the species' breeding ground. We also saw two common scoters, dark birds which stayed together as if paired. One of them was almost certainly an adult female; the other looked like a subadult male.

I continued to wonder why we came upon no buildings, why no one shouted at us or asked us what we were doing. We saw no human being aside from ourselves.

Had I been alone, I probably would have settled down to painting the baby phalarope. But we all wanted to locate the nests of as many kinds of birds as possible, and as soon as possible, in hope of building up a complete film record and of obtaining chicks of precisely the right age for my drawings.

"How about that peninsula where we found so many scaup nests?" suggested Sewall.

Off we went. As the scaup nests had all held incomplete clutches on June 20, there was little hope of our finding a chick, but always there was the chance of discovering new nests or a recently hatched brood. We had been told in Reykjavík that the scaup nested late in Iceland. Several nests that we had more or less carefully marked we inspected one by one as, escorted by the angry terns and a cloud of midges, we walked to the farthest tip of the peninsula. The hen scaups fouled their eggs with vile-smelling excrement as they flew off. The oldsquaw was not on her nest, but all four eggs were there, completely hidden by a blanket of dark down. The nest of the tufted duck now held a complete clutch of nine eggs.

Purple sandpiper chick a few days old, caught near Dettifoss,
northeastern Iceland, and painted direct from life
July 1, 1958.

MÚSARRINDILL

Young Iceland wren just after leaving the nest.
Painted direct from life at Mývatn,
northeastern Iceland, July 2, 1958.

My feelings about the midges were mixed. The insects were thoroughly objectionable, there was no arguing about that. They crawled into our eyes and ears and inside our clothing. Occasionally we choked on one. Especially bothersome were those which, captured within an ear, continued to buzz just beyond the reach of such pocket-knife blades, birch twigs, and other ear-scraping implements as were available. But there was something soul-satisfying about the realization that the midges did not bite.

Red-necked phalaropes were all over the place—pairs, threesomes, companies of up to five birds, twittering, fluttering about, alighting in the water with audible plops, and twirling about in a great fuss over nothing. We could not understand these phalaropes. Why were the females not laying, the males not incubating? We had found a brood of chicks that very morning, yet here was a whole population of phalaropes, literally scores of birds, that to all appearances had not even started to nest. Two explanations seemed plausible: the unusually cold weather had delayed nesting or caused a wide loss of first clutches of eggs; or all these birds were young of the preceding year just now entering upon the nest-building, egg-laying phase of their first reproductive cycle.

On our way back to the hotel we stopped long enough at a small pond to find a whimbrel's nest. The Pettingills had seen the birds here repeatedly but had not found the nest. Ensconcing ourselves a long way off, the Pettingills to one side at pond level, I to the other side on much higher ground, we found the nest, which was much closer to the water than I had expected it would be. It was among grass and moss only an inch or so above pond level. The four huge, olive-buff eggs were blotched with dark brown. How I would have enjoyed spending the rest of the day with those whimbrels! There was something exhilarating, even inspiring, about the way in which they strode across the rocks, flew back and forth on strong, quivering wings, and varied their sharp calls of protest with bubbling, windy trills.

Before the afternoon was over, I managed to draw the baby phalarope, direct from life as planned; but the tireless Pettingills kept me on the jump. We were to eat our evening meal, I was informed, at Námaskard, the famed valley of the boiling mud pots, so off we went again—eastward this time —past an isolated little house in which we had been told we could take a steam bath, out of the green lowlands up into the brown, between hills whose sides leaked steam, upgrade again, higher and higher, the truck's most powerful gear coming noisily to our aid in the final climb.

Nothing that I had read, no picture that I had seen, had prepared me for the weird beauty of the valley into which we slowly descended. To the left of the road were dirty snowbanks from which tiny streams trickled downward, downward, eventually off to a faraway area green with grass and stands of small birch trees. To the right, on slopes far above us, was the yellow of sulphur, almost as bright as the yellow of mustard flowers, along the lips of narrow openings partly veiled by steam. As we rounded the shoulder of the great mountain, more and more of the valley became visible. The slopes below us were rusty red except for a line of intense blue at the very bottom. Suddenly the jets of live steam came into view, cloud-white and roaring away, for an instant calling to mind a great factory or roundhouse. The largest jet, the one farthest to the right, resembled smoke from a huge locomotive climbing the slopes from the other side. The iron horse itself was not yet visible, but at any moment it might appear, snorting, puffing. We turned right off the main road and climbed to a shelf from which we could look directly down on the whole amazing spectacle. Now, with a feeling akin to fear, we realized that steam was issuing in little wisps all over the slopes about us. The smell of sulphur was strong. For any sort of plant life—for leaf or stem or blossom—we looked in vain.

For me the most evil-looking, the most awe-inspiring, of all these surface activities of the earth's hot interior were the boiling mud pots. As I walked toward these pots, which were almost circular, I had a feeling that I had somehow, somewhere, lost touch with reality. Much that we had seen at Mývatn had seemed strange, but all of that was believable enough as compared with this. There were moments when I thought I could hear underground echoes of our footfalls. I could not bring myself to approach the pots closely; instinct seemed to warn me that even my own puny weight might be too much for the earth's thin shell. Hardest of all to understand was that the ground on which we stood was reddish brown, light in shade, whereas the pools of hot mud, whose level was only a few feet below that of the dry, hard earth surrounding them, were dark gray, almost black. Endlessly the thick-walled bubbles rose, took hemispherical form, ruptured, formed, ruptured, formed, plopping, slurping, plopping, slurping, sinking back into the scalding fluid matrix whence they continued to rise. The bubbles reminded me of navels. "Navels of devils" was a phrase that crossed my mind. "God help us all" was close to what I kept thinking. It was very nearly a prayer. Even as I write, at this moment a long, long way from Iceland, I recall the strange

Navels of Devils / 81

excitement of standing there, the powerful fascination of it all; and I wonder now, as I did then, whether a human being could ever see enough of those mud pots to lose his awe of them. Could a child reared near them come to regard them as commonplace, to take them for granted? Could they ever be anything but terrifying? We were told that an American soldier had fallen into one of them and died there. What a way to die!

My special chore was finding fresh water for dinner. I started my search gladly, for I wanted to get away from the mud pots and the smell of sulphur. The blue streak at the bottom of the valley proved to be not water but a layer of smooth clay, dry as a bone. Eventually, off to the north, not far from the nearest fringes of shrubbery, I found a shallow stream of snow water. What I dipped up was heavily laden with silt, but it had no taste of sulphur.

XIII

"Mrs. Greengate"

FOR ME A QUESTION demanding as prompt an answer as possible was this: Who owned the garden spot we had been calling "the stacks?" Never could I think of that place without longing to be there. Nowhere about Mývatn had we found such a variety of birds as lived there; nowhere else had we seen the Barrow's goldeneye and common scoter. The remarkable lava formations, which resembled the remains of a huge causeway or aqueduct, were unlike anything we had seen in Iceland. I could not recall having stood in a single spot in that whole "stacks" area that had not been scenic and exciting. I continued to suspect that it was a government-owned park of some sort, perhaps an arboretum in which trees imported from afar were being grown experimentally.

When we set off for "the stacks" on the morning of June 24 the air was sharply cold and the mountains off to the south and east were white with fresh snow. As we drove southward, but without a word to the Pettingills about the matter, I resolved to find the owner of this land, to obtain permission to work there. Already I had stolen a baby phalarope, and I had dire designs on every bird species that nested thereabouts except possibly the redwing. The Pettingills didn't know what it was to feel guilty; no blood was on their hands. But I, innocent looking though I was, for I carried no gun, was a killer. I had set out to make a series of drawings showing the natal plumage of the many waterbirds which bred in Iceland, and the *juvenal* plumage of the half-dozen or so passerines which bred there. These drawings were part of a long-range study of the birds of the whole circumboreal area. I had long ago learned that drawings made from museum skins would not do, for in these specimens the colors of the fleshy parts were hopelessly faded and the plumage patterns were frequently distorted. No, the only truly satisfactory drawings were those made directly from living models. The models had to be chosen with care, too, for I wanted to record not some postnatal or postjuvenal plumage stage but the natal plumage exactly as it was when the chick first became dry after hatching, and the juvenal plumage exactly as it was when the chick first learned to fly. I had long since convinced myself that this painting work was important. I carried with me an official scientific collecting license obtained through the good offices of Finnur Gudmundsson; but realization that the work was important, and that it had full governmental approval, did not change the fact that I was a killer, a sort of wolf in lamb's clothing.

Inside the green gate once more, the Pettingills and I walked to the merganser's nest, found that the eggs were not hatched, and followed the shore line northward to higher ground. At the edge of a sixty-foot cliff we looked down on placid water in which idled a scattering of goldeneyes, among them some gorgeous drakes, several pairs of common scoters, and two pairs of Slavonian grebes. The drake scoters were rich black—every one of them was in full breeding feather. Looking at them carefully through our glasses, we noted that there was a small yellow spot on each bill. We observed that when the pairs of scoters flew past or rose from the water, the hen invariably was in the lead.

The Pettingills had more than enough to work with. Leaving them, I walked upslope, reaching the road leading in from the gate, and followed this thoroughfare to its very end. Before me stood a well-built house, half-hidden by trees; beyond were a strip of garden, a fringe of birches, and the lake. Emboldened by determination which had been growing stronger hourly, I marched up to the door.

My first knock brought a little dog bouncing happily round the house toward me—its ears laid back, its body wriggling at the edge of ecstacy, its tongue ready to confirm what its nose already had told it—that here was a stranger whose looks were dubious but whose smell was certainly of mud, grass, birds, and other thoroughly worthwhile things. I have never been given to patting strange dogs on the head, but this one—one of the very few dogs I had seen in Iceland —was obviously expecting some show of affection. Presently I heard footfalls, the door opened, and there stood before me as kindly looking a lady as I had ever seen, a good-looking lady too, who to my relief understood English perfectly. Without the slightest difficulty I explained *most* of what we three Americans were up to, and she, gracious soul that she was, told me that we were more than welcome, that birds had always interested her, that she would be glad to know of anything "special" we might happen to find on her place. I spoke of our interest in the Barrow's goldeneye. "Oh yes," she said, "that is the duck we call the *húsönd*, the house duck. It is very common here." I longed to tell this lady, a widow named Gudrún Pálsdóttir, exactly what I planned to do. I longed to take her completely into my confidence, to tell her that I could not paint birds direct from life without catching them, that some of these very models I would preserve as specimens; but she was so very kindly, and my own plans seemed so brutal by comparison, that I could not bring myself to explain them.

"Come, I will show you one of the duck nests," said she. And she led me up a steep mound that covered a cellar of some sort to a cluster of small conifers, under one of which was a widgeon nest. There the hen was, trim, utterly motionless, bright-eyed as only an incubating duck can be, her body covering all but the outermost rim of the nest. I almost touched her before she fluttered off. There were eight eggs.

"There's a nest in the garden, too," she continued. "It is a duck of another kind, the kind we call the *stokkönd*."

This time the nest was under the broad leaves of a big rhubarb plant. The bird was used to the comings and goings of human beings and did not fly off until we were very close. It was a mallard, and twelve eggs were in the nest.

Telling my new friend that I would bring the Pettingills to the house as soon as I could find them, I departed in high spirits. I was beginning to feel at ease. After re-examining the eggs in the widgeon nest, wondering how close they were to hatching, I continued to climb the hill east of the house and within a short time had found two more duck nests—a mallard's at the edge of a thicket and a gadwall's under a birch that stood in the shelter of a huge rock. On the hill's very top at last, near the little rock cairn we had seen from the highway, I looked in vain for the Pettingills. Overhead were a hooting snipe and a singing meadow pipit. Off to the south an excited pair of redshanks were calling. I directed my binocular that way and instantly realized that a certain bright spot in the landscape was Sewall's shirt. That indefatigable bird observer was in a thicket, his binocular lifted. He was watching the redshanks, doing his best to ascertain what all their yammering was about.

When, presently, I walked down the slope, approaching him closely enough for conversation, I heard him say, "These birds have been yelling at me all morning. There's *got* to be a nest here!"

I hastened to a tree about fifty yards away and sat down, not very sanguine about the whole business, for I had devoted hours, literally hours, to watching redshanks at Reykjavík and not one of the birds had led me to a nest or chick. Hardly had I ensconced myself when Sewall, running as swiftly as I'd ever seen him run, made for a certain spot, swooped, and came up with a kicking redshank chick of exactly the stage I needed.

I could hardly believe my senses . . . but here was the chick itself, right in my hand! Examining the lovely creature, whose legs and feet seemed disproportionately big, I felt great happiness and relief. At Reykjavík I had failed to find a chick despite the astonishing abundance of the species there. Here the redshanks were decidedly rare, yet we had been lucky enough to find a chick of exactly the right age.

"Mrs. Greengate" / 87

Jubilant over this unexpected bit of success, I led the Pettingills to Gudrún Pálsdóttir's house. From the gracious lady we received an armful of rhubarb stalks and an invitation to coffee that afternoon. I strove to be mannerly, but my mind was on the redshank drawing that was already in the making. How could I manage to make the chick stand still? How could I force myself to draw its legs and feet as big as they actually were?

As we walked back to the truck, my mind was on the chick, but I added my bit to the conversation. So the lady's name was Gudrún Pálsdóttir. This was her summer place. She had a house in Reykjavík also, on a street called Bólstadarhlíd. We could not bring ourselves to calling her Gudrún, for that seemed too familiar; yet we could not call her Mrs. Pálsdóttir, for that was not correct form in Iceland. She had been married, to be sure, but that did not change the fact that she was first of all Gudrún, daughter of a man whose first name was Páll; marriage had not made her a "Mrs." of any sort! Affectionately, and in a sort of American desperation, we decided that our name for her would be "Mrs. Greengate." The name seemed to fit, for the gate had never been anything but gentle and hospitable.

The redshank chick strode along, three or four inches to each stride, in a manner like that of a crane. I marveled that it never tripped on its own toes and that it could move swiftly across the table top or along the window sill without making the slightest noise with its feet. When I lifted it and set it down, it remained motionless for a split second before striding off. I managed to draw it in this give-me-a-second-while-I-make-up-my-mind attitude.

Late that afternoon we went back to Gudrún Pálsdóttir's.

Not far from the house was a stand of small rowanberry trees in which we hoped to find a nest of some sort, perhaps a redpoll's. While we were moving from tree to tree, inspecting each, Eleanor flushed a meadow pipit barely out of the nest. It fluttered off in a straight line, dropped exhausted, and allowed itself to be captured without the slightest squealing or struggling, but it was so hard to see in the grass that for a long time we feared we had lost it altogether.

Now were we confronted with a very real "public relations" problem. We were expected at the house within a few minutes. The truck was fully half a mile away. We had no box into which we could put the pipit. The coat I wore had big pockets, and in one of these the pipit nestled down comfortably. I had no pin with which to fasten the pocket shut. Leaving the coat outdoors without pinning the pocket shut meant certain loss of the pipit. So into the house we went, pipit, unpinned pipit-pocket, and all, and no one aside from the Pettingills noticed with what ludicrous care I sat down, kept my voice low and even, took my coat off, and hung it over the back of my chair. Conversation was pleasant and the coffee delightful. Gudrún Pálsdóttir's little niece and two little granddaughters were sweet girls, lovely to look at and charmingly polite. I should have come right out with a statement about the pipit and my need for a box, but I feared that something would be said which would oblige me to let the pipit go, so I played the coward and said nothing, wondering with every burst of laughter whether the pipit would flutter forth, shrieking in alarm. Not a sound did the pipit utter. When, at length, we departed, I was half-surprised at finding it still alive. So silent had it been that I had begun to wonder if it had died of suffocation or hopped out and been gulped down by the dog. I painted it before dark, while the Pettingills were off photographing whimbrels.

The meadow pipit was one of Iceland's really common birds. We did not find it quite everywhere, but it was obviously adaptable to a great variety of habitats. The densest populations lived in treeless grasslands, but scattered populations throve in thinly grassed areas throughout which there were scatterings of trees. We had been told that the merlins of Iceland lived principally on meadow pipits. We were later to observe an arctic skua (parasitic jaeger) carrying a fluttering pipit in its beak. We came in time to think of the pipit as comparable to the lemming in that it was so frequently eaten by predators. Iceland had no lemmings, but the pipit to some extent took that little mammal's place as a basic food item.

XIV

White Fire

BY THIS TIME I had a definite plan concerning the pictures I wanted to paint. Every day, in the lava-rock area along the north edge of which we ate breakfast, we saw many white wagtails, every one of them an adult busy gathering mouthfuls of midges. There certainly was no midge shortage. We judged that the entire adult wagtail population had young in nests, for nowhere did we see a young bird. Repeatedly we looked for nests, but when food-carrying adults flew under rocks, we could not tell just where they went; openings which led between and below the rocks were usually so small we could not follow; and worst of all, there was no telling when a rock might suddenly jar loose. Experience with the wagtail nest at Reykjavík had taught me an important lesson; I was not going to be pinned down again. The wagtail chicks of first broods back at Reykjavík had left their nests long since; but Mývatn was colder than Reykjavík; spring had been slow in reaching this northeastern part of Iceland.

So greatly did I enjoy the quiet colors and dainty ways of the wagtails that I decided I would paint an adult bird, basing my drawing not on a captive model but on pencil sketches made in the field. I would perch my bird on a bit of lava rock and this rock would have some of the beauty I had been enjoying day after day—the beauty of plush-soft mosses, of brittle lichens, of tiny holes and furrows that reminded me of worm or barnacle borings. On June 25 I found myself a fine chunk of rock, lugged it to the hotel room, and painted away for hours, abandoning myself to the minutest detail, knowing full well that my subject matter had indoor lighting, but comforting myself with the realization that many a wagtail perch was in a cave whose lighting was not unlike that of a window-lighted room. In designing my picture, I made certain that room enough for the wagtail was left at the top. The bird I would draw in later.

When the Pettingills came in from photographing Slavonian grebes, a diving oldsquaw, and that long-suffering pair of whimbrels, they found me elated over the progress I had made with the wagtail's rock, but dejected with a muddy, wholly unacceptable drawing I had made of a clump of tiny pink flowers. I had seen golden plovers feeding near these low-lying flowers repeatedly, and I had in mind a picture which would portray both the plover and the flowers, but this start was a flat failure.

Sewall reported finding a duck nest that had puzzled him. The nest was in willow brush not far from the whimbrel nest we had found on June 23. He thought that the bird which flew from the nest was a scaup, but the three eggs were larger than scaup eggs and their color was not pale greenish-gray but pinkish-buff. All I could say was that I felt sure the nest was not a scaup's.

Sewall had had a wonderful experience photographing the diving oldsquaw. Perched with his camera on the cliff edge not far from Gudrún Pálsdóttir's house, he had been able to follow the bird as it had moved gracefully about, had fed on the bottom, and finally had come up with big eyes sparkling and with water running down its sleek plumage. I had watched many a diving oldsquaw in the American Arctic and knew how beautiful they could be. What Sewall told me reminded me especially of a day in the early spring of 1945 when Sir Hubert Wilkins and I had timed the dives of an oldsquaw in Casco Cove, off Attu, at the western end of the Aleutian chain. Sir Hubert was far more of an ornithologist than most of his friends realized. In dive after dive the bird stayed under almost exactly sixty seconds. Sir Hubert did the timing with his wrist watch. The water was about six fathoms deep. The bird had presumably gone to the bottom at each dive.

At Reynihlíd that evening four fine young Englishmen, Messrs. Cooke, Hill, Roff, and Clase, dropped in for a visit. They were from Cambridge, and they were busy with a study of Slavonian grebes. Thus far they had found 120 nests, many of them so close to shore that it was possible to count the eggs without use of a boat. The men were carrying on this research under the direction of our friend Finnur Gudmundsson.

Next morning I worked an hour or so at my flower drawing, but it became muddier and muddier, the petals lost their crispness, and the whole thing gave me a pain. Knowing that a look at new country would do me good, I decided to walk to a narrow, grassy peninsula I had several times looked down on from the highest land near our breakfast nook. I was still limping, but the last traces of self-pity were being replaced by a fierce determination to *find things*.

In reaching the peninsula, I followed a road through the rough lava, went through a gate, crossed a broad hilltop covered with knee-high timothy hay, and let myself down to lake level. The sky was overcast, the wind not very strong, the flies bad. Once I set foot on the peninsula, my attention was so focused on the bird life that nothing else mattered. "Odd, very odd," I thought to myself as I zigzagged along, avoiding the marshiest spots, "I've looked down at this neck of land a dozen times, never dreaming that it was alive with birds!" Arctic terns circled overhead, scolding constantly and diving at me whenever I drew close to a nest. Phalaropes flitted about, agitated because I had invaded their nesting area. Hen scaups continued to fly up from down-lined nests. Well out from shore, in the main body of the lake, grebes, widgeons, pintails, gadwalls, red-breasted mergansers, and red-throated loons floated idly. Nowhere did I find a scaup nest with a full set of eggs. This was a real disappointment, for I wanted very much to obtain a day-old chick. Nowhere did I see a tufted duck or teal, species of special interest since I had had virtually no experience with them. I continued to wonder how the behavior of the Old World teal might differ from that of its New World congener.

I discovered that what I had supposed to be the peninsula's tip was really a separate island. On this island a good-sized colony of black-headed gulls were nesting. The gulls attacked me savagely as I stood there figuring how far I'd

Teal chick painted direct from life
at Mývatn, northeastern Iceland, July 2, 1958.

HRAFNSÖND

Hen common scoter caught on her nest
near Mývatn, northeastern Iceland, and
painted direct from life July 4, 1958.

have to swim or wade in reaching the nests. Several of the gulls hit me squarely on the head—not hard enough to throw me off balance, but hard enough to show me that they meant business. I tested the water with my hand. It was surprisingly warm.

I had decided to undress when a smallish brown duck scuttled off through the lush grass, followed by five chicks which were just about as fleet of foot as she. I dashed after them, succeeded in separating two chicks from the others, and caught one. They were shovelers, the first we had seen in Iceland, and not a common species. The captured chick kicked violently as the half-submerged mother thrashed about at the water's edge, quacking loudly.

The chick was obviously more than a day old, but it was in complete natal plumage, so I decided that I should paint it. I started back for the hotel. The gulls escorted me for a time, but soon lost interest. The terns continued to badger me as long as I remained on the peninsula. The walk back was dreadfully time consuming, but it was imperative that I return to my "studio." I had long since learned that there was no sense in trying to paint where wind, sun, rain, and flies could get at me.

In my room at last, I felt in my pocket for the shoveler chick. It was gone! For an instant I wondered if I had lost my senses. Then I thought back: yes, I had used both hands in opening the main door of the hotel. I hurried to the lobby and saw what an average guest would surely have called a rat streaking across the floor. It was the chick.

How long I worked I have no idea, but the drawing was virtually finished when the Pettingills came in. Sewall was radiant. His cupped hands held a treasure I had hardly dared dream of—a newly hatched dunlin. "We found it over near the whimbrels," he said, adding, with unexpected depth of understanding, "You can have this one as a specimen. We'll get another for you tomorrow." He knew I had been working hard. He knew I could not tackle another drawing that afternoon and hope to do the subject justice. Said he to Eleanor: "Come look at this shoveler drawing. It looks as if it might jump right off the paper." Exaggeration, of course—but very heart warming.

The Pettingills decided to go to Námaskard for more pictures of the steam jets. Hardly had they departed when word reached me that some water birds which had been caught in the fishing nets had been saved for me. I went to the underground snow cellar across the road, climbed down the ladder, and found there in the half-light a red-throated loon, two hen red-breasted mergansers, a hen scaup, and a horned grebe. I wanted to preserve the skins of these lovely birds, but there was no time for such work. The job at the moment was preparation of the dunlin chick, an exceedingly delicate operation.

Return of the Pettingills was invariably a time of excitement. The doleful report on bad light, bad wind, bad flies, and unco-operative subject matter I had learned to expect, for my beloved friend Sewall was an expert photographer. This time clouds had shut in and a gentle rain had started, making photography utterly impossible. Eleanor's comment was on the brighter side; or her dismissal of the adverse was accompanied by such blistering invective that the circumstances seemed funny rather than tragic. Yes, she admitted, the weather at Námaskard had been truly awful . . . "but wait till you see the grotto where I do the laundering, and where we took a bath!" I knew from the gleam in her eye that the grotto had indeed been something.

Into the noisy, dusty, ponderous but faithful blue truck we piled and started off. The plan was to drive to the grotto. There I would take a much-needed bath and we would also have supper. Bread, butter, tomatoes, smoked mutton, and cake Eleanor had bought at the hotel kitchen. With one last pang over not being able to preserve the birds in the snow cellar, I joined in the hilarity of this new adventure.

How my friends found their way is more than I'll ever know. In the middle of nowhere we left the main road, heading for a certain green field—one of those astounding rectangles of waving emerald brought about by breaking up the surface lava, adding fertilizer, planting seed, and letting dear Nature do the rest. Having found the field, we followed what in an ordinary countryside might have been called an escarpment, glimpsing now and then a bit of evidence that mortals had passed that way, bumped dubiously along for a mile or so, and hauled up suddenly before a hole in the rocks so similar to the thousand other holes we'd been passing that for a moment I strongly suspected that we were lost.

"Go take a look," said Sewall, pointing to the hole. I walked over, still limping a bit, let my eyes adjust to the darkness, and saw way down below me the gleam of water. I walked back to the truck for a towel, clean underwear, and soap; crept cautiously into the hole; let myself down, down, down, ever so carefully; found a flat rock; and took off my clothes. I was chilly and tired. I trembled a little from exertion and excitement. But as I sank into the comfort and warmth of the water, all trouble seemed to vanish. By this time my eyes had become accustomed to the darkness. The grotto led off in two directions. The water was several feet deep, but since I did not need to stand on anything, I clung to a rock with my hands, suspended in this heavenly medium. I rubbed on some soap, but no lather formed. How blissful it was to idle there. The stiffness and vague pain seemed to leave my right leg completely. I wanted to stay there, to stay on, to drift off to sleep if possible. . . .

"Still alive down there?" queried Sewall, a hardened realist known to me since the Churchill days as Sewall the Cruel. "The food up here smells promising!"

So out of the water I climbed, the towel did its work, clean underwear got pulled on somehow, and I returned to mundane things. Dinner was excellent, as always. Conversation consisted of highly palatable gossip, bits of good, wholesome cynicism, discussions of plans, and fun-poking.

The high moment of the evening, indeed, one of the high moments of the whole summer, came unexpectedly as we stood there near the truck. Off to the south, where the sky was leaden above black and white mountains, eight whooper swans appeared, flying in majestically from the west. The whole world was gray, though the drizzle had stopped. Suddenly the setting sun broke through the clouds, the slant rays shot eastward, and the swans glowed like white fire.

XV

Lake of Midges

By THIS TIME we knew something about Mývatn weather. We also knew that, despite the chill air and raw wind, summer was advancing. The reproductive cycle of the birds was now so far along that courtship was virtually over. Recently we had seen drake goldeneyes going through some funny antics and Sewall was eager to record this behavior. We could be sure of seeing goldeneyes at "the stacks"; we could be sure of photographing them if the sun was bright and the air cool enough to keep down the flies. Our plan, then, was to be at "the stacks" so much of the time that when goldeneyes, sun, and chill air arrived simultaneously, we would be there too. We resolved to start work early the following morning (June 27) if the weather was at all promising.

By half-past four we were up, dressed, and on our way. The sky was far from cloudless; for minutes at a stretch drizzly rain fell; but when the sun came out, the colors of rock, vegetation, lake, and sky were brilliant. We left the truck at Gudrún Pálsdóttir's house, carried the equipment to the cliffs nearby, and looked down on a scene of tranquil loveliness worth crossing an ocean to see. Near the foot of one of the huge "chimneys," in water dark with reflections, idled a company of goldeneyes, most of them hens. Off to the left, where the lake reflected only the bright sky, swam a veritable flotilla of goldeneyes, all of them moving slowly closer. Never had I seen so many goldeneyes in one place, and realization that all of these were *Barrow's* goldeneyes made me resolve afresh to observe them closely. They could not have been hungry, for they did very little diving. Occasionally a gorgeous drake pulled back his head, pointed his bill straight up, and kicked hard enough to splash water over his tail, or, moving toward a hen, initiated a chase which ended with disappearance of both birds under water. Sewall ground away happily. The light was perfect and there were very few flies. My own feelings were badly mixed: seeing all these goldeneyes was wonderful, of course, but where in heaven's name were the nests? We had clambered about every cliff we could negotiate, investigating crevices and holes. We had watched hens literally for hours, but never had we seen one flying up to or down from a ledge, hole, or crevice. Was this idyllic spot merely a recreation area? Could this be one of those off years when certain species forego nesting altogether?

As if to remind me that no one can hope to be infallible as a finder of nests, Sewall pointed toward a hole within a few feet of the grassy spot on which I stood.

For a split second I suspected that my friend had long since found a goldeneye nest without saying a word about it.

I looked. There, almost within touching distance, tail out, utterly motionless, was a hen red-breasted merganser on her nest. Many people consider me a good ornithologist. Sewall Pettingill himself knows that I have my points. The cold fact remains, however, that I had walked past, around, or over that nest half a dozen times. I had almost sat on it.

We decided to go after a dunlin chick for me to paint. We had only a few kilometers to drive. The nesting area was a spongy, hummocky meadow a hundred yards from the lake shore. Soon after parking the truck, we heard a long-drawn-out beady trill, a sound reminding me of a high, taut wire strummed by the wind—the flight song of a dunlin. The Pettingills showed me exactly where they had found the chick they had brought in. Here, wearing a head net, I concealed myself as best I could and waited.

I kept both parent dunlins in sight for half an hour, but neither of them went to a chick. Finally, not knowing how else to proceed, I walked to a hummock on which one of the pair had stood for some time. Nowhere could I find a chick. Presently, above the hum of flies, I thought I heard a thin, high peeping. The sound continued. For some reason, perhaps because my eye had detected a slight movement there, my attention was riveted upon a tiny, mottled ball of soft moss not far from my feet. It was the chick.

We drove back to Reynihlíd and I painted until late afternoon. The chick was a difficult subject because the patterning of its head and upper parts was so intricate. Some of the tiny spots looked like silver-gray bits of mica caught in the dark down.

After supper I returned to the peninsula on which I had captured the shoveler duckling. Close to the very spot at which the hen shoveler had so surprised me, I nearly stepped on a mother teal whose entire brood was one chick. Her concern for this bit of fluff was touching. She flew round and round me, quacking loudly, falling into the water, hiding behind tufts of grass, beating her wings. At times she came so close that I could hear her agitated breathing. The chick shot off through the grass, reached the water in no time, and headed straight for the opposite shore, almost running on the surface. I expected it to tire soon, but it kept up this killing pace until it reached the shelter of vegetation about sixty yards away.

At Námaskard, early the following morning, we had a memorable look at a brood of five young ravens, all able to fly well but following their parents about, begging for food. Nowhere at Mývatn had we seen a raven. The noisy family kept to the higher slopes, eventually moving toward the craggy mountains off to the north.

I could not keep away from the spot at which I had seen the mother teal. I continued to wonder whether I had stepped on her nest, crushing most of her brood. I found no teal anywhere, but along a stretch of shore that had thus far escaped my attention I came upon several tern nests and three black-headed gull nests. The tern nests were mere depressions in the ground; but the gull nests were substantial structures, each on its own little islet close to shore, each holding three eggs.

On my way back to the hotel I found the hayfield half cut. The mowing machine, which appeared to be as up to date as any farm machinery I'd seen in America, moved confidently up the gentle slope, felling a wide swath. I was much impressed with the purity of the crop: here and there I could see a flower, but most of the stand was hay.

While walking through a lava area, I saw an adult wagtail fly down between some great chunks with a mouthful of flies. I quickly hid, watched several comings and goings of two adult birds, and decided that the brood was still in a nest somewhere under a certain large rock. The rock was a focal point. Every mouthful of food was carried under it. My search started. The old birds showed great concern, but did not feign injury. As I approached an opening under one side of the rock, a short-tailed wagtail flounced out, its wings brushing my face. Another popped out, using exactly the same route. I tried to follow them but could not tell where they had gone. Again I peered into the opening. While my eyes were becoming accustomed to the darkness, two more young wagtails flew out—each handling itself expertly, not fluttering and bumbling along, but flying strongly up past the rock and around it. Presently I could see the nest, a bulky affair resting on a sort of shelf. A bird was perched on its rim, a well-feathered youngster with tail over an inch long. Catching this chick required all the cunning I possessed—a slow, slow approach plus a final quick thrust of my hand. I had witnessed the fledging of four of the brood. Had I let my captive go, I would never have caught it again.

Before reaching the main road, I made one more notable observation—a wren with food in its mouth. This not very common species we had seen from time to time among the birches. One had sung volubly near our breakfast nook. I wanted desperately to find the wren's nest, but the wagtail drawing came first—now that I had my model.

Before the day was over the Pettingills and I drove for the first time along the north side of the lake. We saw several whooper swans and spent an interesting half-hour watching two men haul in a big trout net. The trout they had caught were wonderful. Sewall took some pictures of the men at work.

XVI

The Grandeur of Dettifoss

AMONG THE SCENIC WONDERS of Iceland are the great waterfalls, the best known of which are Godafoss, Gullfoss (pronounced Goód-li-foss), Skógafoss, Öxarárfoss, Ófaerufoss,
Laxárfossar, Fjallfoss, Háifoss, Seljalandsfoss, Svartifoss,
Hundafoss, and Dettifoss. This listing does not follow an
accepted order of importance. I have no idea which of them
the Icelanders consider the largest, the highest, or the most
beautiful. While we were at Mývatn the most important of
them to us certainly was Dettifoss, for we knew it was not
very far away. We were reminded of this fact repeatedly,
for many of the persons who traveled as far as Mývatn were
on their way to Dettifoss.

We started for Dettifoss on June 29. It took us three days
to get there. Not that we traveled all that time; indeed, we
did all the traveling, both going and returning, on July 1;
but on June 29 we were so determined to start at 4:30 A.M.,

at 6:00 A.M., and at 7:30 A.M., that our remaining at Mývatn seemed a mere delay en route. How dark the sky was, and how cold the air! The rain was not heavy, but it chilled us to the bone. This was *winter* rain. Experienced persons told us that, unpredictable and local though Iceland weather was, the chances were that it would be raining at Dettifoss also; that we would not move out of the storm as we traveled eastward. I confess that for me this was good news. I longed to sleep for a change; so sleep I did, until eight-thirty.

Wonderfully rested, and eager to tackle a new drawing, I suggested that we drive to two nests the Pettingills knew about but I had never seen—the "puzzling" duck nest that had held three eggs on June 25 and a wheatear nest at which Sewall had been photographing the old birds. The duck nest was unbelievably close to the road in a knee-high thicket of willow that was virtually surrounded by water. The hen fluttered awkwardly off as we approached, alighted in shallow water close by, and called hoarsely as she swam about slowly. The seven eggs were a beautiful, lively shade of buff. The hen was only a rod or so away. There was a tiny spot of yellow on her bill. She was a common scoter.

The wheatear nest was about a foot back in a rock in a hole so small that neither Sewall nor I could reach into it; but Eleanor, whose hands were slender, could touch the nest without difficulty and she obtained for me the most venturesome, and therefore probably the largest, of the brood. It was, as most of my models were, so lively that I gave up trying to make it stay in one place. Tethering it by a leg did not help in the least. Models tied down in this way spent most of their time dangling at the end of the string. Putting them into a fruit jar or under a glass bowl never worked, for invariably they crowded against the glass and part of their body had a pressed-flat appearance. This wheatear I held in my hand while I worked out the details of bill, mouth-corner, and eye; then I let it go, allowing it to scramble about while I made pencil sketches as best I could. I believe I am correct in reporting that it never walked or ran at all. One reason I feel sure about this is that all the shore-bird chicks I had thus far painted had not hopped but had walked or run.

A memorable treat of the day was the delicious dandelion greens we had for supper. The most luxuriant dandelion plants we had seen grew at Gudrún Pálsdóttir's place. Great bunches of leaves, pale and succulent, the largest of them about fourteen inches long, grew in deep moss in the shelter of the birches. The buds had not yet appeared. These greens we gathered in great handfuls, and although they cooked down to almost nothing, their flavor was refreshing. We never tired of them.

Again we started for Dettifoss on the morning of June 30, but again the rain forced us to delay. The flies were bad, for the air had warmed and there was no wind. Wondering from moment to moment whether the rain might stop and conditions so improve for photography that we would be duty bound to start off, I stayed within sight of the hotel all morning, observing golden plovers in hopes of finding a pair that had eggs or chicks. These plovers were, it will be remembered, of a different species from that with which I had become familiar in the American Arctic. They were the Old World species, *Pluvialis apricaria*. They seemed considerably more docile than the many American golden plovers (of the species *Pluvialis dominica*) that I had seen at Church-ill, Manitoba, and near Lake Amadjuak on Baffin Island. I knew that the chick of the American species was one of the most beautiful of birds—golden yellow and black throughout its upper parts, with an intricate pattern that called to mind the aureate elegance of the adult in its breeding attire.

What was wrong with me, or with the plovers, there at Mývatn, I continue to this day to wonder. I spent hours with what I believed to be mated pairs on June 30 without finding a nest or brood. The date was not too early for eggs; we had found a complete clutch at Godafoss on June 19. I could not be sure that the Mývatn birds were breeding. They seemed to go about in twos, yet never did one feign injury, and never did I—from places of concealment in cracks in the lava rock—see one go to a nest or chick. I observed the birds at all elevations—on the barren heights several hundred feet above lake level, on the lower slopes, even along the shore itself where the plovers were feeding in grass that had been cropped short by cattle.

It was near some of these half-tame plovers that I became aware of a remarkable geological feature. Along the shore were dome-shaped shells of lava, fifteen to thirty feet in diameter, that I surmised had formed while the rock was still molten—rock bubbles blown up by fiercely hot steam. The broken shells were fantastic beyond belief. Within them the water was crystal clear and utterly motionless. Below them there seemed to be no bottom at all. As I looked out at the lake, I saw more holes that appeared to be bottomless. What a lake! What a country!

While returning to the hotel, I learned an important lesson: cross all lava fences with great care. Wherever livestock are pastured in a lava area, some of the fences are usually built up of pieces of hard, sharp-edged lava rock. The pieces cling together, almost interlocking, staying in place with remarkable fidelity despite wind and rain. But when a man tries to climb over them, they may tumble. Fortunately no lava fence fell down on me. I was not even scratched by the rocks I dislodged. But I learned my lesson.

While making my way along one of these fences, trying to find a place safe for climbing over, I saw a wren with food in its mouth. "This time," said I to myself, "this time I'll find that nest!" And find it I did, after only a moment or two of watching from a hidden position. It was a remarkably compact ball of moss fitted into a crevice in the roof of a sort of cave. The whole place was so dark I had trouble seeing the nest at all, but I could feel the entrance with my fingers, and I could tell from what I touched inside the warm, cozy structure that it was packed with well-feathered young. With my binocular I watched the comings and goings of the old wrens. Both of them scolded loudly with their mouths full of food, and the male occasionally paused long enough to sing a brilliant, tinkling song. The food they brought may have been flies largely, but some items—spiders probably—were larger and longer legged than flies.

This wren was one of the birds I especially wanted to observe. It was the only wren, the only species of the great family Troglodytidae, found in the Old World. How—small, short-winged creature that it was—had it made its way to Iceland? How had it managed to spread across the whole of northern Eurasia? This was the very species I had found breeding in wooded parts of Canada, in the Appalachian Mountains as far south as West Virginia, and at the western end of the Aleutian chain. Never could I forget that first wren I had seen on Attu—a tiny brown bird scampering from rock to rock through the loose snow, a bird that, flitting up the face of a cliff, called to mind a bit of lichen caught in an up-draft. Here was that same species—small, energetic, aggressive—in Iceland. Here, as on Attu, it was strictly non-migratory.

Before the day was over I made a quick round of the nests I had found on the marshy peninsula near our breakfast nook. To my delight I found a newly hatched chick in one of the black-headed gull nests. The chick was perfect as a model for it was too young to stand. It was pale reddish-brown with bold dusky markings.

At 4.00 A.M., Tuesday, July 1, we actually set out for Detti-foss. The sky was almost cloudless, the sun bright, the air so warm that at Námaskard the steam jets were far less spectacular than usual. We stopped for breakfast along the road not far from some basin-like depressions lined with thick stands of scrubby birch. In these isolated patches of low-growing forest a few pairs of redwings were nesting.

On our way to the great fall we drove over a handsome new suspension bridge, passed the little white tents of groups of campers, and negotiated a long stretch of one-way road unique in my experience. This road wound through comparatively flat, not very rocky country. Kilometer after kilometer it was wide enough for only one car, its bed being so deep that climbing out at either side would have been utterly impossible. We continued to wonder how widenings for passing would be marked. There were no widenings. There were no markers. Fortunately we met no one. Had we met someone, who would have done the backing up? I've often wondered.

Barrow's goldeneye chick painted direct from life
at Mývatn, northeastern Iceland, July 5, 1958.

RJÚPA

Rock ptarmigan chick painted direct from life
at Mývatn, northeastern Iceland, July 7, 1958.

The highway signs were so small, so inconspicuous, so amazingly self-contained, that coming upon one of them sometimes gave us a shock. Hour after hour we had traveled toward this much-talked-of waterfall without seeing more than small bits of proof that we were on the right road. Certainly we had been moving in the right direction: no longer were we traveling eastward, we were headed north—exactly as the map indicated. We had been heading northward a long time now. Off to the left we caught sight of a bit of road leading up a rough slope. It didn't look at all like a road leading to a major attraction. Charging noisily along as was our wont, we sped by the junction of the two roads without seeing that important sign—until we had passed it. There it was: the Dettifoss sign post, perfectly upright, neat as a pin, telling us in small, cultured letters that if we would turn left and follow the road, we would see something worth seeing.

Oh, be not fooled by the understatement of the Icelander! The letters of that sign could have been ten feet high and a neon arrow pointing the way could have flashed scarlet, purple, and orange without beginning to do justice to the grandeur that spread before us as we reached the top of that little hill.

I recall that I was driving. I recall that at the highest point, the point from which we could see at last the canyon walls and the white mist cloud, a golden plover scuttled off to the right as if from a nest. I recall noticing a sharp curve to the left not far ahead. I recall stopping with great suddenness and saying something in a loud and positive voice. The Pettingills laughed uproariously. Burlesquing the scene, they quote me thus, "I don't care what anyone expects of me, I'm not driving one foot farther. This is as far as I'm going to drive, you hear me?"

I must have been badly on the defensive, for it was obvious to all concerned that even had I wanted to drive another rod or two I could not have done so. For a long, long way ahead the little road was buried under heavy-looking snow several feet deep. It was awful the way the Pettingills laughed. What I said or the tone of my voice must have been very funny.

We left the truck right there. It was in no one's way. Eager to see the fall, we hurried down the slope. Soon we were at the edge of a canyon whose walls rose hundreds of feet above the churning river. The walls were of columnar basalt, the columns vertical. Upstream we saw part of the fall itself, but the veil of mist and its lovely rainbow were what held the eye. The canyon wall created an odd illusion. Well up from the bottom there was a horizontal dark streak. So similar were the columns above and below this streak that those below appeared to be a reflection of those above, making the streak look exactly like a waterline. Repeatedly was I deceived by this, despite my knowing that the rushing river at the canyon's bottom was incapable of reflecting images so perfectly.

As we stood looking down into the canyon we suddenly realized how very birdless the whole place was. No chirp, no whistle. Only the roar of the fall! The wildness of the scene called for ravens, but no raven was there. We decided to go back to the hilltop to see if we could find the plover again. We found the nest without difficulty, within a few feet of the road. There were four eggs. The incubating bird feigned injury beautifully when we first put it off, and Sewall made haste to set up the camera; but when we tried to in-duce the bird to repeat its performance it failed us badly.

When we returned to the canyon, we saw below us, flying slowly upstream, a bird of the sea—a fulmar petrel. Actually we were not very far from the north coast of Iceland and a trip from the river mouth to the fall was no trip at all for such a strong flyer as this. How tiny it looked, and how strange to be looking *down* at it. A few moments later we saw a hen red-breasted merganser flying downstream. She may have left a nest high on the canyon wall. Four birds thus far—the two golden plovers, a fulmar, a merganser. No-where a raven, nowhere a gyrfalcon, nowhere even a merlin! The scarcity of bird life was beyond belief.

Knowing that I could not help with photographing the falls, I decided to see what I could find in the wild-looking country off to the east. I walked back to the main road and on for a mile or so, finally coming upon a pair of ringed plovers which must have had a nest in a flat, gravelly area. This was, all in all, as completely barren a place as I had seen in Iceland. Not a birch was in sight. The only vegetation I could find was scattered tufts of grass, clumps of lichen, and an occasional flower. I continued to expect some fine bird to appear, a falcon or owl, perhaps a ptarmigan. But the little plovers were all that I could find anywhere. Disappointed to say the least, I returned to the river.

When I reached the truck and surveyed the slopes below me, all was as I had expected it to be except that the man Pettingill, ensconced on a rock at the very brink of the fall, had his great camera, tripod and all, with him. How he got it there I shall never know. But there he was, pipe in mouth, grinding away as usual. I saw all this detail through the glass.

The Grandeur of Dettifoss / 113

Not far behind him was the faithful Eleanor. I could not help admiring the sheer determination that had driven Sewall to take this precarious position, the sheer strength that had got him there.

Presently I joined the Pettingills, finding Sewall exasperated with the fickleness of the rainbow. In my not quite humble opinion there could easily be too much rainbow in a film, but friend Sewall thought otherwise. What he wanted was so many hundreds of feet of rainbow that he could choose only the very best—or maybe he had in mind sending little reels of rainbow as Christmas cards. Long since I had decided that there was no explaining the ways of photographers.

When I left the Pettingills, I headed southeastward, up over a low cliff to wilder, more barren country than ever. When I was properly hidden from view, I stretched out and took a nap. The sun was so warm that I pulled off my heavy shirt. When I started walking again I found myself thinking about statements I had heard and read of the purple sandpiper's nesting in the most barren parts of Iceland. "Barren," I thought, "what anywhere in the world could be more barren than this?"

It is an incontestable fact that within half an hour of entertaining this thought I flushed from the rocks a shore bird that darted off with a sharp cry, alighted for an instant not far away, and returned to circle near me. A purple sandpiper! I inspected it again and again through the glass, followed it, lost it, lay down and waited for it, walked in big circles until I found it again. Without a doubt the bird belonged here. It had a nest or chicks here. It never quite feigned injury, but it would not leave the place.

Finally, backing up and hiding behind a chunk of rock, I kept my eye on the bird at a distance of perhaps a hundred yards. The sandpiper ran a few steps, shook its plumage, and stood erect, eyeing me all the while. Not far from it there was a blurred spot of dark brown, a moving spot. The blur was a chick. Running as I haven't often run, I pounced on the chick, hardly believing my senses. Never before had I held a really "new" purple sandpiper chick in my hand. It was precisely what I wanted for my painting.

When I told the Pettingills that I had something special cupped in my hands, they looked interested but skeptical. When I said "purple sandpiper," they thought I was fooling. We had spoken of a purple sandpiper chick a hundred times since coming to Iceland.

We took the chick back to Mývatn in one of Eleanor's galoshes. It was exceedingly difficult to draw for its legs were strong. Repeatedly it jumped from the table top across to the window sill, a jump of several inches.

Supper was late. We noticed that the flies were bad; we had been bothered very little by flies at Dettifoss. Suddenly a cold wind sprang up, the flies disappeared, and fog crept in over the lake from the south and west.

XVII

The Drive to Húsavík

IT WAS COLD AND FOGGY at six o'clock the following morning. Hoping that the wren brood had not yet fledged, I walked to the nest and gently touched it. The chick which popped out flew with surprising rapidity straight toward the base of a rock about fifteen yards away and bumped into the moss. Luckily for me, it did not scuttle into a crevice. By watching the old birds as they brought in food, I learned that at least two of the brood had fledged before my arrival and that others were still in the nest. The two birds that had left the nest first were several rods apart. As I walked back to the hotel, I noticed that the air was warming up and that the flies were bothersome. Between seven and eight o'clock the fog lifted and the flies became really bad. I started drawing the wren immediately after breakfast—even as the Pettingills, more encouraged by the brilliance of the sun than discouraged by the flies, set off after pictures.

The wren, like the young wagtail I had painted not long since, was surprisingly strong. In color and shape it was the very counterpart of an adult, except that it had a prankish, mischievous facial expression. Wisps of natal down clung to the plumage of its nape.

The Pettingills happened upon a brood of recently hatched phalaropes. Only the male parent was in attendance, and so intent was he on caring for his progeny that when Eleanor held one of the chicks at ground level in her hand, the father bird ran up promptly, fluffed out his under plumage, and brooded the chick as if there were nothing in the least extraordinary about having part of a human being underfoot. He even allowed himself to be caught! The episode was the more remarkable in that a complete motion picture record of it all was obtained.

Everyone was in a fine mood at luncheon for we all felt sure that the morning's pictures would turn out well. Light conditions had been perfect and the breeze had become strong enough by ten o'clock to keep down the flies. For Sewall the fly problem was not so much a matter of achieving personal comfort as of taking acceptable pictures. He could endure the pests when they crawled over his hands and face (he used a head net at times), but when they alighted on the lens or danced in a cloud between camera and subject matter, they were beyond enduring, beyond patience, beyond philosophy. Some of our meals in the truck were made thoroughly unpleasant by the flies until we learned that by shutting the windows we could panic the pests. Now, as if seized by claustrophobia, the flies seemed to forget all about us, rushed headlong for the glass, and milled about in desperate confusion trying to get out, and we could wipe them

The Drive to Húsavík / 117

downward with an old rag or piece of paper, crushing them by the hundred.

Flies or no flies, the brightness of the weather brought all the farmers out to cut hay, and a sight to see were the big mowing, scattering, and raking machines moving busily about in every field. All this fine, up-to-date equipment seemed to be performing perfectly. The machines were usually run by men, but occasionally a teen-aged boy or girl managed a rake or scatterer. Many a man in charge of a machine held a little boy or girl in his lap, and the faces of man and child shone with health, pride, and contentment. Children seemed to be everywhere—along the edges of the fields, in the recently raked stubble, in groups in the middle of the road. Haying time! The flies were bad when the wind died down, but always there was the wonderful smell, the activity, the feeling of accomplishment, the fun of riding to the barn on one of the big, shaggy, aromatic loads. The work continued all day and far into the night, for the weather was fine. Apparently the hay did not need to be cured very long if the sunlight was strong: it lay for a while as cut, then the scatterer kicked it about, and finally the rake gathered it into piles which were forked onto wagons by hand.

After finishing my wren painting, I went to an area I had come to think of as peculiarly mine—the narrow neck of land half a mile beyond our breakfast nook. Luck was with me. Halfway out toward the tip of the peninsula, I came upon a hen teal and four tiny chicks. When the hen burst from the grass at my feet, I feared I had stepped on the nest; but as she circled for return, I heard high, shrill peeping and saw the chicks darting ahead of me. The mother kept at a safe distance, now rising into the air with quick wingbeats, now flopping to the ground and dragging her feet and tail as if injured. Her breathy quacking must have sounded a warning, for suddenly every chick stopped running and the peeping ceased. Had I not had my eye on two of the brood I might have lost them entirely. Kneeling, I examined them closely. They were crouching low; their heads were stretched out in front as if in resigned acceptance of an unkind fate; but their eyes were bright and wide open.

When I picked up one of the chicks, it peeped loudly. Instantly the rest of the brood took up the cry and off they all scampered, precisely as if the mother's stop-in-your-tracks command had automatically been canceled.

I started back for the studio at Reynihlíd immediately, for a baby teal was a bird I had especially wanted to paint direct from life. As I left the scene of the capture I noticed that the terns, which had been diving at me fiercely, suddenly ceased their attack, changed their strident *tearr* cry to a sort of chatter, and rose rapidly en masse. Even as I noted the brightness of their sun-struck tail-feathers and marveled at the way they kept together, a gyrfalcon appeared in their midst—cruising along with its dark eyes on the shore line. The terns did not attack, but they milled about as if sensing that their very closeness might bewilder this ancient foe. As the great bird moved off, I could not keep from my mind a gray battleship escorted by a lot of little sailboats.

The teal chick was one of the liveliest, most attractive creatures I had ever worked with. I was amazed by the swiftness with which it could race off from a squatting position, and by the abruptness with which it could come to a dead stop.

The day ended on a solemn note. When the Pettingills came in, Sewall announced that the starter of the truck was misbehaving. We had joked about the awful noise "Big Blue" invariably had made in getting under way. We had grumbled about the dust which had continued to get in no matter how tightly we had closed the windows. We had groused about the complexity of the gears, the crash that accompanied every shutting of the rear doors, the impossibility of stowing the spare tire properly. But all in all the truck had been wonderfully faithful. Time after time it had got us there. Never had it failed to make the grade. Never had the engine heated up, or the fan belt snapped, or a tire gone flat. "It can't be the battery," said Sewall. "The battery has been charging properly right along. It's the starter. All day long I've had trouble with the starter!"

To show me how feeble the starter was, Sewall tried it. There was a wheezy sound, a sort of death rattle. He tried again, pushing hard. There was no response, none whatever.

Assured by Sverrir Tryggvason that we could be pushed or towed in case we needed to start the motor, we learned that the closest garage was at Húsavík, some fifty kilometers to the north. "There's a good man there who'll fix it for you," he said. "But once we get you started, be sure you keep going! Better wait till Thursday so the milk truck can give you a push if you need it! The milk truck goes to Húsavík on Thursdays." The words had an ominous sound.

The following day, July 3, we were to have luncheon with Gudrún Pálsdóttir. "We'll have lichen soup and trout," our friend had said in issuing her invitation.

From six to nine o'clock that morning the fog was so thick it was oppressive. I preferred not to recognize its existence, so stayed indoors, working at specimens and notes. Shortly after nine o'clock, seemingly all within a few minutes, the sky brightened, the fog withdrew into the mountains, and there lay our big, bright, silvery Mývatn, just as big, bright, and silvery as ever.

Since the truck would not start, we set out for "the stacks" afoot. The first three or four kilometers weren't so bad, though I noticed that I had difficulty keeping up. The fifth and sixth kilometers had me wondering if I'd make it, though of course I said nothing. During the seventh kilometer I was astonished by Sewall's speed. I had never before thought of him as being a *disagreeably* fast walker. During the eighth kilometer, it was Eleanor who had me dumfounded. How could she do it? Why didn't she object, or suggest a bit of a stop, or complain of Sewall's obnoxious pace? So used were we to driving this stretch of road that we repeatedly found ourselves farther along in imagination than we actually were. "No, that's not the hill I thought it was. The hill I had in mind must be farther along," was someone's comment.

Finally, an hour and a half late and gaunt with hunger, we arrived. Our hostess had guessed that something was wrong. How cordial she was! And how understanding! She had heard of starter trouble before.

The meal was delightful from start to finish. The lichen soup, known as *grasa molche*, was wholly new to us in both flavor and texture. Down very rapidly went the wonderful Mývatn trout, the Carlsburg ale (from Denmark), the new potatoes and the chives, as if we had promised not to arrive, but to finish, by a certain hour. Gudrún Pálsdóttir was a person of culture and of wide experience. Conversation never lagged. Concerning such dubious matters as the pipit theft I preserved a stony silence.

Our friend was good enough to drive us back to the hotel,

a gesture for which I was deeply grateful. The evening we spent watching wheatears that had a nest in the lava rock and gulls that flew in one by one to alight on the roof of the old Lutheran church.

Friday, July 4, was glorious enough. We got the truck started with a brisk tow; we reached Húsavík without trouble; we found there a mechanic who from the very first impressed us with his friendliness, directness, and jubilant know-how. He spoke no English, but his smile said plainly enough, "Just you leave that truck with me. I know exactly what's wrong. I'll have it all fixed for you in less than no time!"

I see I have got badly ahead of my story. The drive to Húsavík was anything but uneventful. It is true that we never once let the motor die; it is equally true that never, in all our driving in Iceland, had there been so many good reasons for stopping. First there was the whimbrel's nest, which had to be watched lest the chicks all hatch and get away without being photographed or sketched. And the scoter's nest, which presumably held a complete clutch of seven eggs. And the mother mallard with her big brood in the middle of the road. The mallard considered the dry, airy, open place hers, not ours, so she was averse to leaving. Then there was the great whooper swan and its little gray cygnet so close to the road that we longed to get out the cameras and try for pictures. Finally, there was my inevitable failure to watch for approaching cars at one of the highway-widenings designed and marked for passing. I have no idea to this day what the Iceland law requires in such a situation; but I knew I had forgotten to look ahead properly, I felt that I was somehow to blame, so I did the backing.

While "Mr. Húsavík" was removing the old generator

brush, which had been worn almost to oblivion by that powerful abrasive, volcanic ash, we three Americans enjoyed the bright roofs, the clean streets, and the two fine piers of this northernmost of Iceland's larger towns. Eleanor bought quantities of food at a store. The mechanic wanted American money in payment for his work. He was going to Copenhagen, where the purchasing power of our dollars was great. I wish we had given him more dollars than we did.

The drive back to Mývatn was memorably pleasant. The starter sang as we stepped on it. There were bright flowers, fields of new-mown hay, and literally hundreds of water birds to enjoy. The whimbrel eggs, though pipped, were not yet breaking open.

Since the day was still young, I decided to capture—if I could—the scoter whose nest we had last visited a few days earlier. I knew exactly where the nest was, for I had taken careful note of its position with regard to the road, the water's edge, and certain fence posts. When I stepped through the willows, moving in toward the sitting bird, I half expected her to fly off noisily, fouling the eggs. But she did not budge. I knelt quietly, lifted my right hand very slowly, brought it down swiftly on her neck and upper back, and had her. The nest held seven eggs.

The scoter was not difficult to handle. She was a beautiful creature, almost velvety dark brown all over without markings of any sort except for a touch of yellow on the bill near the nostrils. Her tarsi and toes, including the webs, were black. Her eyes were very dark brown, almost black. We drove back to Reynihlíd as quickly as possible. I wrapped the scoter in an old towel and set to work on a portrait of her head and neck. I worked about two hours and was well pleased with the drawing. But my joy probably did not equal that of the scoter, who, tossed high into the air from the road in front of the hotel, behaved for a split second as if incapable of movement, then whirred off toward the lake.

XVIII

"Many's the slip . . ."

FOR THREE MORE DAYS we worked at Mývatn. They were exceedingly busy days, for by this time we had scores of nests under observation, eggs were hatching right and left, and the lake was alive with broods of baby ducks and grebes. I was desperately eager to find a Barrow's goldeneye nest, for, of all the ducks we had seen, this species continued to intrigue and baffle me most. We wanted to find a harlequin nest, too, but the harlequins all lived along the Laxá River and driving to them seemed to take too much time. As for the whooper swans, graylag geese, red-throated divers, and great northern divers that nested in the Mývatn area, we had seen so little of them that we didn't even know which direction to take in looking for their nests.

Our failure to obtain a widgeon chick thoroughly annoyed me. This species we had been seeing daily and we had found several nests, some of which we had visited often. We had seen at least one hen with a brood out on the lake. Time after time along a certain stretch of shore we had flushed a flock of handsome drakes—a flock that had grown steadily larger as summer had advanced. Yet here we were at the end of our stay and we had not yet even had a good look at a chick.

There were two other species about which I felt especially bad—the scaup and the tufted duck. The scaup was downright abundant at Mývatn, but so late had it been in starting its egg laying that I had long since given up hope of seeing a chick. The tufted duck seemed to be common too, but the one nest we had found was not close to hatching, so here again I had given up hope of seeing a chick.

The goldeneye nest problem we started to solve on July 5. That morning, as we looked down from the cliff near Gudrún Pálsdóttir's house, we saw not a scattering of drake and hen goldeneyes but three hens with broods. There they were, along the opposite shore possibly three hundred yards away, one with eleven chicks, another with eight, another with six. Even through our glasses the chicks looked dark, but as they bobbed along following their mothers, the white of their cheeks gleamed brightly in the sun.

Sewall wanted photographs, of course. But he knew how desperately I needed one of those chicks, so down we climbed to the rowboat which had been put at our disposal and off we started. We soon learned that although the chicks were very young, they dived well; that when they went under, they instantly became invisible despite the clarity of the water; that chasing the chicks by following the mothers was utterly futile, for once the brood was scattered there was no telling what the mothers would do or where they would be.

Whole broods went under at once. Then up the chicks bobbed, here, there, yonder, sometimes near the mother, often a long way from her. Eventually we cut two chicks off from the others, thought we had them headed nicely toward shore, and promised ourselves that they would soon be ours. Oh, many's the slip 'twixt such a promise and a chick! The two ducklings went under. When they came up, several rods apart, we went after the nearer. It promptly dived. We looked around wildly, but in vain, for the other. Glad enough for a rest, we stopped rowing; and, keeping a sharp lookout, we eventually saw one chick, by itself, well out in the lake. We started after it only to see the other come up almost exactly where the boat had been. Thus it went for half an hour, for an hour, for an hour and a half. Finally, by dint of singling one chick out, forcing it to shore, watching it closely, rowing in the right direction as it went under, and seeing it come up among roots under a grassy bank, we caught it as it took refuge in a hole. It was beautiful beyond words—very dark gray, almost black, with bold white markings. Its big feet were wonderfully soft and smooth. But the unbelievable thing about it was that it was not even out of breath. Sewall and I were just about done in.

Back at my room I painted away at the baby goldeneye, a wonderful model so long as I held it in my hand. But the problem of the nest continued to bother me. That very morning we had seen three broods of goldeneyes. Those broods represented three nests, not one of which we had found. Where could all these goldeneyes be nesting?

My painting was well along when Sewall came in with a snipe he had caught. The bird probably had flown into a wire, for its right wing had almost been torn off. I welcomed this chance to sketch a snipe from life, and was glad to see the bird running about vigorously on the floor; but when, presently, I laid the duckling aside and tackled the snipe, I sensed that I was not giving this new subject undivided attention. I finished the sketch perfunctorily, knowing full well that the problem of the goldeneye nest was dominating my thought. If those ducks nested in holes, as the books all said they did, then what sort of hole did they choose—a crevice in the rock, a burrow in turf, a cavity back among roots? Could the birds possibly nest in chimneys? Might *that* be the reason the Icelanders called them *húsönd*—house ducks?

Back to "the stacks" we went, all three of us in full agreement that the goldeneye nest would have to be found. Sewall was sure that he had obtained satisfactory photographs of broods, for the light had been good. By this time we had crawled about certain cliffs so much that we felt sure there were no nest holes there. We decided to use the boat, to row out to "the stacks" themselves. We'd always wanted to have a close look at them anyway.

Sewall and I climbed about the bases of "the stacks" as best we could. The huge masses of lava rose straight up from the water to a height of sixty or seventy feet. There were crevices aplenty, but no holes that seemed to be right for nests, and certainly no duck flew out. Thorough scrutiny would require ropes, and ropes we had not.

We decided to row southward below the cliffs about which we had so often clambered. As we were passing between two little islands, a hen goldeneye flew suddenly from the left, just in front of the boat and not very high in air. Something about the way in which she skidded into the water and swam about with head moving slowly back and forth told us that she had flown from a nest. Not since we'd been at Mývatn had we seen a goldeneye behaving in this way.

The spot from which I guessed the bird had flown seemed to be covered with knee-high vegetation. As I stepped out of the boat and scrambled up the slope my heart was pounding more from excitement than from exertion. "Be patient," I kept telling myself. "By all means be patient! Be thorough! This is no time for halfheartedness!"

And sure enough I found the nest—back about twenty inches at the end of a hole whose entrance was hidden by grass and pretty pink flowers that reminded me of what we called wild geraniums in America. The hole and its entrance were about a foot in diameter. The six large, warm, pale-blue eggs lay in a thick bed of grayish-white down. I couldn't be sure how the hole had been made. Assuredly no mammal had dug it, for there was no pile of earth at the entrance and, besides, no fox would be likely to establish a den on a little island of this sort. A flattish rock formed the roof, and I could feel a rock at one side, about halfway in to the nest.

Finding this nest led us to believe that we might easily locate others; but when we climbed about the other little island, a few rods away, we found only tufted duck's nests. This second island was like the first except that several large clumps of willow grew on it. We found at least a dozen nests there, every one a tufted duck's. Two of them were only about five feet apart. The ducks seemed to be nesting almost colonially, in the manner of eiders. We identified the hens with care as they flew off. Not one of them had the boldly white face of a hen scaup.

"Many's the slip . . ." / 129

Before calling it a day, we visited the whimbrel nest. Each of the big eggs had a little hole in its side, and we could hear a chick pecking and peeping inside one of them, but the two ends of the shell were not yet being forced apart.

The following day (July 6), while Sewall was busy with his photography, Eleanor rowed me quietly to the island of the goldeneye nest. I took off my shoes, got out noiselessly, and stalked that bird literally on hands and knees. The broken-down vegetation told me exactly where I had been the day before. I had no way of knowing that the bird was on her nest, but I had to assume that she was. Near the entrance to the hole at last, I heard scratching sounds. Falling forward, I grabbed the hen just as she was spreading her wings.

Once more luck had been with me. Once more I felt that the impossible had happened. In my hands was a living, struggling goldeneye. Her big, round eyes, which had a genuinely fierce look, were pale, grayish yellow, not rich golden yellow, as I had expected they would be

I got back to my room as soon as I could and set to work. I painted the duck's head twice, the black and orange-yellow foot once. Never did the bird's face wear a friendly, tolerant expression. In this respect was the goldeneye very different from the scoter.

When the Pettingills came in that afternoon, I was discouraged. I felt that I had not done my subject justice. Sewall's sentiments about his own work seemed to match mine. He had had a terrible time with the flies.

Our last day at Mývatn, July 7, was one of the busiest I had ever lived. We knew full well that Mývatn was not the only lake in Iceland about which widgeons, scaups, and tufted ducks nested, but here we knew just where to find the birds; we knew exactly where several nests were; we had been watching some of these nests day after day. All this work we would be obliged to leave half-done, alas!

Not far from Gudrún Pálsdóttir's house I flushed a hen ptarmigan whose behavior clearly indicated that she had eggs or young. She flounced over some little birch trees, alighted with mouth open and wings drooping, and ran about clucking like a broody hen. Nowhere could I find a nest. Not a step did I take without watching exactly where my foot was going down. The one chick that I found was crouching motionless in as unsheltered a spot as it could possibly have found thereabouts. Much as I wanted to find the rest of the brood, and to ascertain whether the father as well as the mother was caring for them, I knew that other work was to be done.

At the whimbrel nest one chick was out of the egg and dry, and the other three eggs were cracking. The nestful would be perfect for photography within a few hours, after another chick or two had emerged.

Across the highway from the whimbrel nest was a marsh we had visited infrequently. Here we trudged about somewhat at loose ends with ourselves, realizing that we would probably never see the place again. Often I had wondered whether graylag geese were nesting in the vast flats off to the south. We had heard geese there several times and on one occasion had seen a small flock grazing in the far distance. Now I wondered about the geese again, wondered pointlessly, for I knew we would never find the time during this last day for walking so far. Oh, the utter impossibility of doing this work thoroughly, of learning anything about Iceland in a single summer!

"Many's the slip . . ." / 131

The reverie was broken by an explosion of wings as three hen widgeons sprang up from a thicket about twenty feet in front of me and a great company of chicks, some newly hatched, some several days old, rushed pell-mell for the tall grass at the water's edge. I had come to think of myself as something of a cripple, for I usually walked rather slowly and sometimes limped; but on this occasion I must have lost every vestige of self-pity, or of histrionics, or of whatever it takes to make one limp, for Eleanor insisted that I turned into a wildcat. Dashing forward, I caught first a large chick, then two small ones. What a handful! And what a peeping! I kept one of the small ones, went back to Reynihlíd, and, telling myself not to work so hard that the portraits would look labored, I painted first the ptarmigan, then the widgeon. The ptarmigan sat motionless in my hand as if convinced that if only it stayed that way it could never be seen by its enemies. Not so the widgeon!

The colors of the ptarmigan chick were of great interest to me. I was surprised to find no lemon-yellow tone in any part of its plumage. In this respect it was strikingly different from the chicks I had seen and obtained in the eastern American Arctic (Baffin Island) in the summer of 1953. Since adult Iceland rock ptarmigan closely resembled adults of the two subspecies inhabiting Greenland and the one found in eastern parts of the Canadian Arctic Archipelago, some taxonomists, including Finnur Gudmundsson himself, had come to believe that the rock ptarmigan reached Iceland from the Canadian Arctic by way of Greenland rather than from Spitsbergen or continental Eurasia; but I could not help feeling that until we knew more about the color of Greenland chicks we would do well to reserve judgment. The Ice-

land chick certainly resembled the illustration of the ptarmigan chick in *The Handbook of British Birds* far more closely
than it did the Baffin Island and Ellesmere Island specimens in my collection. Had I been obliged to base my decision wholly on the color of the chicks, I would have called
Baffin Island and Iceland birds two *distinct species*, for the
Iceland chick was gray or grayish buff in general tone, the
Baffin Island chick yellow. No one had advanced the idea
that the natal down of the rock ptarmigan was two-phased;
certainly the chicks I had seen on Baffin Island were all yellow-toned, and Finnur Gudmundsson had informed me that
he could not recall ever having seen a yellow-toned chick in
Iceland.

The rock ptarmigan is Iceland's only galliform bird. Records had been kept since 1864 of ptarmigan exported from
the island as game. Finnur Gudmundsson had studied these
records carefully, finding that in 1871, 1880, and 1891 the
species was exceedingly abundant. After a severe "crash"—
a period of extreme scarcity—in 1893-94, there had been a
steady increase in numbers until another peak of abundance
had been reached in 1902. From that time on, ptarmigan had
continued to be common until 1920. In 1910 there had been
a slight falling off, but no crash had occurred and two ten-
year cycles had thus overlapped or merged. The crash in
1920 had been shocking, since everyone had come to feel
that the population was stable. Within four years the species
had again become common, but since 1920 peaks of abundance had come not at the turn of the decade but in the
middle of the decade (1924-27, 1935-36, 1945, 1954).

The fact that the ptarmigan of Iceland repeat, decade after
decade, this rhythmic increase and dropping off is interesting

and of considerable economic importance, but the *why* of it all is what puzzles and fascinates biologists. The cyclic life of some animals is common knowledge. Almost everyone is familiar with the periodic abundance of the cicada known as the "seven-year locust." The cyclic life of lemmings has been studied intensively and the climb of populations of these rodents from virtual zero to saturation is known to require about four years. Since lemmings are so widely distributed throughout the Arctic and since so many Arctic predators are known to eat them, the lemming cycle is widely regarded as a sort of basic cycle on which the cycles of all other Arctic animals depend. But here was an Iceland bird whose cyclic life could not have been brought about by, or influenced by, a lemming cycle, for Iceland had no lemmings. Before the advent of man, about one thousand years ago, the island had no rodents or small mammals of any sort, and the three rodents which had unintentionally been introduced by man (rat, house mouse, long-tailed field mouse) had never become numerous enough to provide much food for predators.

In Finnur Gudmundsson's thought-provoking paper on ptarmigan cycles, he had described Iceland as "an area eminently suited to studies of cycles in nature. It is a geographical unit of moderate size and it has not as yet been much affected by human activities. It has a poor flora and fauna and its ecological conditions are consequently much simplified. It is inhabited by only one gallinaceous bird and the population of this species is subject to violent cyclic fluctuations. The cyclic population changes take place simultaneously throughout the country and, owing to their magnitude, they can be easily followed with fair precision. The combination of all these factors tends to make areas like Iceland better suited to the study of cycles and their causes than areas where the conditions are more complex and where the number of variables is larger."

Toward evening clouds spread over the sky and a light rain started. During supper we were appalled by the swarms of midges that rose from the grass along the whole lake shore. So dense were the swarms that they resembled columns of smoke rising from a prairie fire. We could not help being thankful that we were safe inside the truck, with the windows shut.

The day was not yet over. While I was writing notes and packing specimens, the Pettingills visited the whimbrel nest and took the oldest chick for me. Half-crazy in my determination to set down some sort of record, I sketched away until past midnight. But I wasn't worth much. Neither was the sketch. In disgust I tore it up.

XIX

A Successful Drawing,
A Remarkable Museum, "Surprise Bridges"

THAT LAST NIGHT at Reynihlíd was not very restful. Disheartened by my failure with the whimbrel chick drawing, I scrutinized the ptarmigan sketch and widgeon sketch closely, decided they were good enough to save the day, set the alarm for half-past three, and went to bed. The baby whimbrel peeped so loudly that I could not sleep, so, putting it into a cardboard box, I took box and all to bed with me. The peeping stopped as soon as the chick became warm and I slept soundly for what seemed to be about five minutes.

When that ferocious half-past three jangle sprang at me from the clock I instantly perceived that there was light enough for work, so I got up, found a fresh piece of three-ply water-color paper and squared away. I longed, I almost groaned, for coffee, but coffee at this hour would have involved unlocking the truck and finding kerosene, starter cubes and matches, not to mention the likelihood that the

Primus would have to be cleaned and that after all this fuss I would find myself, an hour or so hence, sipping a tepid liquid greenish-gray in color as well as in taste. Perhaps it was just as well that I had no coffee, for even without a stimulant I seemed to be drawing everything about twice life-size. Finally I settled down to steady work and finished an acceptable sketch.

About eight o'clock the Pettingills appeared. So voluble were they in praise of this, my latest work, that I felt sure they had agreed to cheer me up. After breakfast, I was told, we would be on our way.

We stopped long enough along the south shore of Mývatn for a look at the tufted duck's nest we had found on June 20. The nine eggs had by this time been incubated about eighteen days. The embryos were not by any means fully developed, but I continued to hope that by some miracle we would find a chick. The hen jumped off, fluttered out a few yards, slapping the water with her big feet, sank to a swimming position, and paddled slowly back toward us, growling hoarsely. Not one of the eggs was pipped; but sitting on them, very pert looking indeed, was a goldeneye chick a few hours old. Two days before, at "the stacks," I had handed Sewall an egg from the goldeneye nest. He had put it in the tufted duck's nest to see what would happen.

It seemed impossible that we should cross the heights between Mývatn and Akureyri without at least one escapade, but we threaded those narrow bridges and negotiated those hairpin curves without batting an eye. A notable bird seen west of Mývatn was an arctic skua with white underparts—the first light-phased arctic skua we had seen. Passing the golden plover nest at Godafoss required forbearance and re-

A *Successful Drawing,* . . . / 137

solve on my part. I knew full well that we would take the side road to the fall if I so much as mentioned that nest. The Pettingills had heard my daily lament over our failure to find a golden plover chick at Mývatn and Dettifoss. They knew very well how important that chick was to me. What I told myself as we sped by the Godafoss turnoff was this: Our job is to see as much of Iceland as possible. An hour's delay at Godafoss may mean a whole day of delay at Reykjavík. Perhaps, if the gods are with us, we'll find a golden plover chick somewhere else.

So on we went—through Akureyri, up into the cloud-hung high country and down again, through Blönduós, eventually to a junction of roads where, had we turned left, we would have continued to retrace our way. But we turned right instead, traveled northward a short distance, and stopped at Glaumbaer, a remarkable museum, a sort of national shrine, near an old church. The museum was actually two rows of sod houses joined side by side in such a way as to form a single sprawling, one-storied structure. Several sections, each with damp earthen floor, had all manner of old rusty tools, fire places, and cooking utensils in them. A section with elevated wooden floor was without furniture but the walls were covered with hundreds of photographs—most of them of men, a very few of women. These people were notable farmers of the district, among them some of the original owners of the many farmsteads that had been established early in the nation's history. The sections nearest the highway—those in front, so to speak—were filled with furniture including built-in bedsteads, cradles, spinning wheels, lamps, hangings, and books. We wrote our names in a big guest book before we left. Sewall took photographs, but the light was not very good.

Back we went to the main highway. Again we climbed. Presently we passed the high lakes in which we had seen red-throated divers a few weeks before. The narrow valley was familiar but the snowbanks we had seen were no more. Down, ever down we went, never very far from the rushing river. At Fornihvammur at last, we failed to convince the faucets that we needed hot water, the door of the bathroom on the second floor was marked neither *Karlar* nor *Konur*, there seemed to be no keys for any of the bedrooms, and no meals were being served, but we were grateful all the same for shelter. It is an odd fact that I, who have a good memory for things I have enjoyed eating, cannot remember much about our evening meal. I believe we drove down to the river, that sweet little river of foam and swift water, and ate in the truck. Wet snow was falling. I seem to recall that a deep pool near us shone for a while with the incredible blue of a morpho's wing, but turned to a rich, deep violet-gray before the meal was over. I was so sleepy that what I thought and felt had the quality of dreams. My bed at the hostelry was hard; that I knew when I sat on it. But a good look told me it was the best bed I had ever seen, and nothing about the blissful hours I spent there proved this judgment wrong.

On our way to Reykjavík we came suddenly upon a little bridge spanning a narrow canyon. It was one of those "surprise bridges" so characteristic of Iceland. Way down, a hundred feet or so, was the stream. For a long way before reaching the bridge the driver could see the road stretching off ahead. What he could not see, until he was all but hurtling into space, was that the road turned sharply to the right at the canyon's rim, then sharply to the left across the bridge, then sharply left again, then hard right—four sharp turns in quick succession. The instant we had made the crossing I sensed Sewall's gathering enthusiasm. He had been thinking about a bridge of this sort a long time.

"This is something we've got to have," announced he.

So, whether the delay would keep us in Reykjavík a day longer or not, whether I were ever to get my golden plover chick or not, I took the part of the driver. Sewall climbed about with his camera until he found an angle from which the whole procedure would look properly awe-inspiring, and shouted for me to go ahead. No rehearsal was needed. I stayed in the road and on the bridge as directed. The scene shows the truck moving along confidently enough. The face of the driver does not show, alas.

We made one more major stop before reaching Reykjavík, this time following a side road to Medalfellsvatn, a lake several kilometers from the highway. In the river which rushed down from the lake the Pettingills had seen harlequins at the end of May, but we could not find the ducks now. In a great flat not far from the lake, a marshy area covered with lush grass, we came upon several pairs of black-tailed godwits, a species I had not seen since June 12. From the behavior of these fine shore birds we knew they were nesting, but search though we did, and thoroughly, we could not find a chick or nest.

The godwits were noisy and bold. The minute we stepped off the road, walking toward them, they flew to meet us. As we trudged about the meadow at least one pair accompanied each of us; but when, binocular in hand, I tried to hide in a thicket on a bit of high ground, up to eight birds gathered round me. When a bird alighted close by I noticed that calling invariably was accompanied by a lowering of the head— as if considerable effort were required in producing the sound. The flight song, which was given only infrequently at this late date, was a rapidly repeated *wheater-wheater-wheater*; the call given from the ground resembled the phrase *tewy-too*. The birds were rich reddish-buff on the head, neck, and breast, mottled brown and black on the back, and white on the belly, flanks, and tail coverts. The bill was long and very slightly upturned. In flight the white at the base of the tail and the white bar in each wing were very noticeable.

In Reykjavík we devoted two hours to washing clothes and bathing, went to Gildaskálinn for dinner, and joined Finnur Gudmundsson in a pleasant evening aboard the *S. S. Caronia*, a handsome ship which had been in the harbor that day.

XX

An Unforgettable Welcome

AFTER ONE MORE DAY of visiting laundries, buying supplies, caring for correspondence, and having a pleasant party with Sigrídur Einarsdóttir at her apartment, we set out again—this time for a little island off the north coast of Snaefellsnes, an island called Melrakkaey (pronounced Mel-rock-kay-ee), the Island of the Fox.

Snaefellsnes was one of those words that for a while I thought I would never be able to pronounce; but when our friend Finnur explained that *snae* (pronounced snī) meant snow, *fells* mountain, and *nes* (nĕs) peninsula, I began to get the hang of it. Out at the great peninsula's farthest tip was a famous glacier—Snaefellsjökull. But I am getting ahead of my story.

Traveling as we did, with food, sleeping bags, extra clothing, and professional equipment in the truck with us, we could stop whenever we wished. The day (July 11) was bright,

Lutheran church near the village of Vík on the southern coast of Iceland. The austerity of the landscape is characteristic of Iceland.

The Barrow's goldeneye nesting ground at Mývatn (Midge Lake), northeastern Iceland. The author (left) and Sewall Pettingill on a cliff in "the stacks" area.

Skógafoss, one of Iceland's most beautiful waterfalls.

Dyrhólaey, or Door Rock, near the village of Vík, on the southern coast of Iceland.

Sewall Pettingill (at camera) and Páll Steingrímsson photographing gannets on Hellisey, one of the islets of the Vestmannaeyjar.

Snaefellsjökull, a glacier in western Iceland.

One of Iceland's great glaciers as seen from the air. The photograph was taken just east of Mt. Hekla.

Lighthouse near Dyrhólaey, or Door Rock, along the southern coast of Iceland. The dark flat land is the breeding habitat of the great skua.

so when, after rounding a mountain and starting the long drive inland to the head of Hvalfjördur, we saw below us a great gathering of eider ducks, I was not surprised when Sewall expressed a desire to see what he could do taking pictures. Hundreds of the birds, most of them adult males now losing their high plumage, were standing along the edge of a low peninsula. The name of the spit was *Hvaleyri,* Whale Spit or Whale Peninsula. A whale may once have been stranded there.

Hardly had the Pettingills started down slope with their heavy equipment when I heard distress cries from two golden plovers. The birds paid special attention to the Pettingills for a time, then flew upslope toward me. They crossed and recrossed in front of me, never feigning injury, but making perfectly clear that they were excited and annoyed. Suspecting from long experience that one of the birds might return to the nest if I completely hid myself, I climbed into the truck. The plaintive crying ceased almost at once; then one bird flew downslope a hundred yards or so, the other upslope about the same distance. As the latter alighted, I saw another plover running toward it. At first I thought that the mate had flown up from below the road; then I realized that this new bird was not quite full grown, that its head was still down-covered. Here was another bit of evidence that the nesting season was well advanced, another forewarning that despite all the attention we had given this common species, we might not obtain a newly hatched chick.

Marking as best I could the spot at which I had seen the young plover, I started up the slope. I ran for a way, but soon was out of breath. Using the glass, I found the parent bird and was surprised at its being so close. Then I saw the young one again—far up the mountain and running fast. The ease with which it traveled amazed me. It seemed almost to be flowing uphill! I was surprised that it did not fly, for it seemed to be almost as large as an adult. Capturing that chick, whose wings were not quite strong enough for flight, took just about all the determination (and wind) that I had. It was not of the stage I wanted for my series of paintings. But I needed a specimen, so I killed it, got out my taxidermy kit, and finished the skin about the time the Pettingills returned to the truck.

Our next stop was at the godwit meadows we had visited two days before. Again we walked back and forth through the grass but found no godwit chicks. We did find a snipe's nest with four eggs, and this gave me a feeling of hope that I hadn't had for some time. If snipes could nest as late as this, why not the golden plovers also? Another find was an old godwit nest with part of an eggshell in it. The shell was olive-brown, blotched with black on its outer surface.

At the junction of the highways near the village of Borgarnes (accent on the first syllable, please) we took the road leading northwestward. With a vague pang I realized that I would probably never see Akureyri or Mývatn or Dettifoss again—those wonderful places that had been such a real part of my life. There was something so absolute, so final, about this choice of roads. Why couldn't we drive back to Reynihlíd and go on watching scaups and tufted ducks until we had *that* job finished?

On, on, hour after hour we drove, never for an instant out of touch with majesty—the majesty of shining lakes and great white swans, of mountains rising abruptly from the meadowlands like huge cathedrals, of distant glaciers gleaming in the sun. No wonder the people themselves had something of majesty about them. How could they be otherwise with such a homeland as this? There was beauty of another sort, too—the gentle beauty of cottongrass dotting the marsh-lands, of colts romping about the vast, unfenced pastures, of whimbrels alighting airily, holding their wings high above their backs just before folding them.

Near a pond in the low country we saw a pair of arctic skuas, one of the birds dark all over, the other white under-neath. This was the second light-phased arctic skua we had seen in Iceland. Most of them seemed to be dark wherever we went.

The road turned abruptly northward, straight for the mountains. Soon we were looking down upon the meadows we had found so delightful, climbing the cathedrals whose lofty spires we had so much admired an hour before. The highway had been built well. There were smooth upgrade stretches unlike any we had experienced on our way to Mývatn.

We reached the highest point, started downgrade, and there before us lay the sea again. This time it was the great inlet known as Grundarfjördur. A town off slightly to the right was Stykkishólmur. Long before reaching the town, we turned left, heading straight into a lava area that from the very first glimpse had us thinking of the moon's surface. The long road to Setberg, our destination, a farm near the Island of the Fox, was a good road, every foot of it; but the part that led across the lava bed was a series of dips, climbs, and sudden curves, the like of which I had neither seen nor dreamed of. He who laid out this road must have had forti-tude and patience indeed; or, perhaps, accepting the topography philosophically, he had said to his crew, "Just put it anywhere. One place is as good as another!"

I had the pleasure of driving some of this wildly tortuous road, and I recall with what relief word went round that it was about time for supper. We pulled off onto a narrow bit of grass bordering a noisy brook and stopped. Knowing that the truck was off the road, that we were doing nothing and going nowhere for a while was a blessed relief.

Our supper spot was at the very edge of the lava bed, and I noticed that the brook flowed not out from the lava but down the steep slope of the mountain just south of us. The road skirted the lava bed even as the brook did. On the far side of the brook grew shaggy masses of a low plant that apparently did not thrive anywhere in the lava. This resembled the spicy-flowered cassiope that I had learned to love in the American Arctic, but I was not sure that it was the same plant. In any event I was much impressed, as I walked about, with the abundance of small, light-gray lepidopterans that seemed to inhabit it. All of these insects looked like butterflies. Now Iceland was said to have no butterflies, so the idea of finding a thriving population of them excited me greatly. I managed to run down about fifty of the insects while Eleanor was preparing supper. To my regret, almost to my disgust, I found that every blessed one of them had the antennae of a moth. Too bad I did not have a net. The specimens were much the worse for wear by the time I had caught them, so I did not try to save any of them.

During supper we listened for birds, not one of which we had seen as we had come through the lava. Far above us on the mountain we heard a whimbrel and a golden plover.

These two species were assuredly among the commonest and most widely distributed of Iceland's birds.

When our road left the lava bed, it closely followed the fjord's shore. Our hearts skipped a beat as we looked ahead, for the mountains rose almost vertically from the water and there seemed to be no room for a road anywhere at their base. With some trepidation we drove through a sizable stream. We had no choice. The road entered the water and emerged, neat and dry, several rods upstream, the only trouble being that between entrance and exit the whereabouts of the thoroughfare was anybody's guess.

On we went, a steep slope, almost a cliff, to our left, the sea a few feet to our right. I took comfort from remembering that this was not a region of extreme tides, that the sea was not in angry mood. Where had the materials for the roadbed come from—had they been hauled there, or had they accumulated, century after century, by erosion and wave action?

One fact about the highway reassured us: nowhere was there so much as a hint of side road. This was the correct route; there was no other. At long last, about ten o'clock in the evening, we arrived at Setberg. The farmstead's fine house was close to the sea. Here lived the Reverend Magnús Gudmundsson, who had been informed of our coming. Not many kilometers off, across a little bay, was the fishing village called Grafarnes. We wondered whether anyone at Setberg would be awake at this hour.

The welcome we received I shall never forget. Magnús and his family were obviously happy to see us. Yes, Melrakkaey, the Island of the Fox, was not far away and thousands of birds were there. Getting there would not be difficult. A boat from Grafarnes would take us over and bring us back. The weather might very well be bright on the morrow, for the season had been dry, but there was no telling. Drinking coffee, we sat in the comfortable living room enjoying each other hugely. My eyes wandered from the exquisite lace curtains, crisp and white, to the oil paintings and the bits of sculpture. I noticed in another room long rows of books. I listened eagerly to the comments of Magnús, a thoughtful man, a scholarly man. Oh, the joy, the thrill, the excitement of being in Iceland, of becoming acquainted with the Icelanders!

XXI

The Island of the Fox

A STURDY BOAT, with skipper and mate, came for us early next morning as arranged. The day promised to be fine. As we moved our gear to the water's edge, we noticed several arctic terns overhead, some moving from the sea to a slope bright with flowers just back of the house, others from the slope straight back to sea. The incoming birds each held a little fish crosswise in its beak. Magnús told us that the colony had nested there for years, that the chicks were hatching now. The old birds were used to human beings, but they scolded perfunctorily, especially when one of us made a move toward the nesting area.

There was no pier, and, since the boat could not quite reach shore, we were obliged to choose between the discomfort of soaking wet feet and the ignominy of being carried aboard. Be it recorded that we were not carried far.

On our way to Melrakkaey we saw a white object in the

water: a dead common murre, floating breast up. I fished it out and shook it off, finding it to be an adult in excellent condition. I put it carefully to one side, planning to skin it when opportunity offered. As we drew closer to the island, we began to realize why we had been advised to come here, for the place was alive with birds. Puffins were flying about, not in flocks but in a sort of swarm. They were not very wild, and single birds often alighted near us. When a swimming bird happened to be dead ahead, the skipper enjoyed seeing how close he could come to hitting it with the boat. He never came at all close, of course, but the bewildered puffin turned this way and that as if unable to make up its mind, then swam frantically for a short distance, finally diving with a little splash or flying off with a patter of wings audible above the sound of the engine. How those birds amused us! Especially those which dived when pressed very close. These sometimes returned to the surface right alongside, looking at us with a comical twinkle in their flat gray eyes and swimming toward us as if to make clear that they had not been trying to escape in the first place.

For a time Melrakkaey appeared to be low and of even topography, but as we moved closer, we realized that the shore all the way around was clifflike, and we saw why it was important that we make our call in quiet weather. Nowhere were the cliffs very high; there was nothing quite awe-inspiring about them; but the nearer we drew to them, the more we wondered where we were to be put ashore. Now big glaucous gulls, with no black anywhere in their plumage, came slowly out to meet us, staying high and calling *kah-kah-kah* in a deep voice. Below them circled the much smaller kittiwakes, whose wing tips were black. Fulmar petrels glided silently past, some of them almost within touching distance. Not far from the boat a black bird of snaky appearance suddenly rose to the surface, its hooked beak pointed strongly upward. After glaring at us with its green-blue eyes, it opened its wings a little and went under again—a shag. As the cliffs began to throw back echoes of our motor, puffins poured down from the island's top by the thousands. Oh, there were birds here; our friend Finnur certainly had been right about that!

Very little sea was running, but putting us ashore was tricky enough. Certain low flat rocks were at the foot of the only slope up which human beings could climb without the help of ropes. Here we got off, the men were good enough to carry our gear to the top of the island, the skipper found a baby puffin for me to draw, off the boat went, and we were on our own. The skipper would return for us in about fourteen hours.

Melrakkaey had been known to the Icelanders for centuries, but for us it was a new world. I suspect that the Pettingills were just as exhilarated—and just as bewildered—as I. Here we stood, on the much-talked-of Island of the Fox at last! All at once there were a hundred different directions from which to choose, a weird, raucous, dissonant symphony to interpret, a low organ point of whirr and flutter to adjust to. An odd smell in the air was not wholly that of tidal flats or seaweed. If we walked at all, it had to be upward, that was obvious; but why walk at all? Why go anywhere? Why not stay right here the whole day through—observing, contemplating, marveling at a single phenomenon—the abundance of life? Puffins were decidedly the commonest of the several species we were seeing. Puffins seemed to be everywhere.

They did not move about in flocks, but great numbers of them were now swimming together not far offshore. Suddenly, impelled by instinct which seemed to make itself felt simultaneously throughout the whole population, they began their return to the island. The hissing roar produced as the beating wings struck the water was vaguely ominous, like the noise of an approaching squall. Soon the routine of coming and going was back to normal. The incoming birds, crossing, recrossing, constantly, endlessly, hung a kind of openwork skein across the sky.

Recalling that there was work to do, we made a swift reconnaissance. The island's whole top seemed to be turfy. A broad slope near the landing spot was thickly covered with stiff, knee-high shrubbery. So honeycombed with puffin burrows was this thicketed area that walking was difficult, if not downright dangerous. Wherever we went, puffins shot forth a short way ahead of us, spreading their red feet wide apart when turning, when putting on the brakes, or when making a landing. Some of them groaned in their strange way. The departing birds went out to sea or alighted at the edges of cliffs not far off and stared at us quizzically.

Believing that the puffins had all been routed by our crossing of this special nesting ground, I began investigating the nest holes. Into burrow after burrow went my right hand, back, back, back as far as I could reach, the fingers exploring hopefully for an egg or chick. By the time I had investigated six burrows without finding a thing, without, in fact, being able to feel the end of a burrow, I marveled that the skipper had obtained a chick so promptly. Refusing to admit defeat, I tried again, felt a sudden tap, then a savage nip between thumb and index finger, and decided against further searching. I had had fair warning. It was high time to get back to drawing. For drawing I needed fingers more than I did a second chick!

I cut such a ludicrous figure as I stumbled back to our gear that Sewall, using a telephoto lens, took pictures of me. With these he intended, I feel sure, to convulse future audiences with laughter, for he did not advise me to walk carefully. I have never seen these pictures, but Sewall has decided not to use them. His "actor," instead of looking funny, looks like a helpless drunk.

The baby puffin the skipper had found for me was soft, utterly helpless, and adorable. It made me think of one of those pudgy ogres in a Swedish cartoon. Though not quite shapeless, it looked as if evolution had been leading it headlong in that general direction for quite a while. It was dark gray all over except for the white on the middle of the belly.

The puffin chick was a good model, for it made no attempt to run away. But I found working in the sun and wind trying, to say nothing of the lice that climbed slowly up my legs as I sat in an old gull nest, or of the liquid contributions showered down from the adult puffins as they sped past. I decided I would have to move. Fitting myself into a niche at the foot of a perpendicular rock face, I squared about until I had the sun at my back and the painting in shadow. The drawing progressed well enough. I worked at it an hour, giving it close attention. Suddenly, allowing my eyes to change focus, I looked toward the sky, and there, on the edge of the rock above me, stood a row of sage-looking puffins, each with its head turned sidewise, looking down at me.

During this painting session I made an interesting discovery quite by chance. Every five minutes or so I heard a thin,

The Island of the Fox / 153

high piping, a sort of squeal that I failed to recognize though I had frequently heard the same sort of sound in the American Arctic. Happening to look up at just the right moment, I saw a black guillemot come out of a hole near the top of a cliff about fifty yards away. As it squealed, it opened its beak wide, displaying the gorgeous vermilion mouth lining. This was the welcome to the returning mate in whose beak were several limp fish. The fish were for the chicks. Prolonged squealing accompanied the combined return and departure, the change-over of the sexes at the nest.

We explored the west side of the island, and to our surprise found several fulmar nests. A few of these were in remarkably accessible places. One, in particular, was on a gentle slope just below the island's top, alongside a big bunch of grass. The old bird flew out as I approached, and there was the chick—a little, grayish-white, shaggy-looking thing four or five inches long, waving its wings, thrusting its head forward violently, opening its mouth wide, spewing foul-smelling oil at me.

This time I took my outfit to the nest and painted the chick without removing it. Once the chick had become accustomed to me, it quieted down beautifully.

To change occupations I decided to skin out the murre, a handsome creature of velvet-soft head and neck plumage. I could not find a clue to what had caused the bird's death. Having very little cotton with me, I stuffed the skin with dry grass from a gull's nest. I was shaping the specimen, wrapping it with a handkerchief so that it would dry properly, when Sewall shouted that he had something he wanted me to see. I stumbled over and, conversing across a chasm about forty feet wide and fully as deep, I learned that he had just seen a young glaucous gull on the rocks somewhere between me and the sea. I started in the direction indicated, and there, sure enough, was a good-sized young gull, still downy all over, but not quite in the natal stage I had hoped for. I approached the chick closely, forcing it to the very edge of the cliff. I fully expected it to leap off, thus killing itself in avoiding capture, but instead it looked inquiringly at the rocks far below, then in about the same way at me, and crouched, suffering itself to be picked up without a struggle.

This time I tethered my model. There was no other way to keep it near me and at the same time allow it to stand normally. The portrait turned out fairly well. A detail of the eye interested me: the pupil was milky blue, not black. While I was painting, an adult gull stood so long in one place not far from me that I tried painting it, too, direct from life. I worked rapidly, laying in sky, sea, and distant mountains broadly. The bird was utterly lovely. The white of its head and neck and the pale pearl gray of its mantle fairly shone in the sun. The heavy bill was yellow, with an orange spot near the tip of the lower mandible. The legs and feet were pinkish flesh color. The shadowed parts of the white under-plumage were almost as blue as the sea. Nothing was wrong with the model or with its setting; but the drawing was amateurish and fussy, no good at all.

When I took the young gull back to its cliff edge, Sewall called to my attention several shag nests that clung precariously to the walls of the chasm. As a group these could be seen to better advantage from his side than from mine; but when I sprawled on the rocks and looked down through a fissure, I beheld the rich green shine on the plumage of a brooding bird only six or eight feet below me. I could see the jaunty, forward-curved crest, too, and the wonderful gemlike eyes. When the bird saw me it began hissing and croaking, its long neck writhed, its wide-open beak framed the livid yellow mouth lining, its gular sac spread and vibrated in a manner calling cobras to mind, and, despite my objective appraisal of all this well-known behavior, I found myself pulled back, back, back to prehistoric times. The puffins, for all their oddness, could be contemporaries of mine, fellow citizens. But not the shags. The shags were living remnants of a past buried deep in the rocks. They were creatures of yesterday.

The kittiwakes were nesting in chasms too, on sheer cliffs somewhat tucked away from the wind. Some of the nests were side by side on ledges, just far enough apart to prevent the brooding birds from tearing each other to pieces with their strong beaks. With my glass I could see that some of the nests held chicks of exactly the stage I needed; but we had no ropes, and, too, I was beginning to feel that any further drawing I might do that day would be unacceptable.

Before we left the Island of the Fox, we visited the north side, crossing en route an area covered with long grass, some of which had been flattened by wind. In the grass we found two or three recently hatched eider broods and a mallard's nest, full of eggs. On the island's north side a small colony of great black-backed gulls were nesting.

At Setberg once more, we reported that our day had been highly successful. Magnús seemed glad to have us back and asked us to dinner. The children, in high glee, grabbed rakes and raced for the tern colony followed by their dog. The terns rose in a spangled cloud, shrieking and screaming as the children, picking their way carefully to avoid trampling eggs and chicks, walked about waving their rakes to keep the terns from hitting them. It was a pretty sight. There was something so natural about the children's enjoyment of the birds. But fancy having a tern colony in your back yard!

Dinner was memorable, not only for the excellent food but for the beautiful linen and silverware, the spirited conversation, the common ground we so frequently found. One of Magnús' relatives was to attend Cornell University in the fall. I told what I knew about the important Icelandic library at Cornell, and about my good friend Professor Halldór Hermansson, who had had charge of this library while I had been in Ithaca. When the dessert turned out to be rich, smooth, genuine ice cream, I could not believe my senses. The trip from Reykjavík had been a long one; the road through the lava bed had been incredibly tortuous; we had wondered whether we would ever find Setberg; and here we were, in Setberg, *eating ice cream!*

XXII

Drekkingarhylur—The Drowning Pool

WE LEFT SETBERG the following morning (July 13) before anyone else had got up. This time we were headed for a big sea-bird colony and a pair of red-throated divers farther westward on Snaefellsnes, the former on the south side of the peninsula in the general vicinity of Snaefellsjökull, the latter on a small lake close to the main road leading westward between Snaefellsjökull and the sea. To reach this western end of Snaefellsnes, we would have to backtrack through the rough lava almost to Stykkishólmur, then southward across the high country to the lowlands on the peninsula's south side and westward into high country again.

Snaefellsjökull had by this time become a familiar landmark for us. In clear weather at Reykjavík we had seen it repeatedly. From the window of my room on Birkimelur I had often rested my eyes looking at it, wondering whether it would be difficult to climb. At midnight it had sometimes looked like a low, roseate cloud, for the vague grayness of its base seemed to separate it from the mountains and the sea, pushing it well above the horizon.

Today, as we drew closer and closer to it, seeing it sometimes for half an hour at a stretch, the gentleness of its slopes seemed ever the more remarkable. Even when scrutinized with the glass, it seemed to be wholly without crevasses. The more I saw of it the more I wondered at its remaining frozen all summer long. Why did it not melt away?

The beauty of the great glacier was enhanced by certain less spectacular, less formal elements of the landscape. I recall being thrilled by the way in which the broad, motionless cone seemed to stand guard over the meadowlands with their bright blue, breeze-rippled ponds, their patches of nodding cottongrass, and their families of swans. I could imagine the bleakness of all this during a winter storm, the hostile austerity of the peak in cold weather; but now not even the highest part of Snaefellsjökull seemed quite austere.

When, at length, we looked northward rather than westward toward the big glacier, we began to have difficulties with the unlabeled roads. We noticed that we were approaching Stapi, a little village on the coast, but we could not seem to make the side road leading to this village fit any road shown on the map. Learning the hard way that no road led westward through the village, we returned to the main highway and drove farther west, eventually finding ourselves heading straight for what appeared to be a high, solitary rock at the sea's edge.

The rock reminded me at first of a grain elevator, for its tallness contrasted strongly with the flatness all about it; but as we saw it in greater detail, it began to look like a cathedral or château whose central tower rose above the main body of the structure, overhanging it slightly. Comparing the rock with a building did not tax the imagination at all, for the sides rose vertically and parts of the top were horizontal. Actually there were two rocks, one possibly three hundred feet high, the other much less high. Nothing in the vicinity was in the least like them. I wondered if they might be great chunks of rock that had been hurled in semifluid state from a volcano; but Finnur Gudmundsson informed me that in the opinion of Jóhannes Áskelsson, an authority on the geology of Snaefellsnes, each of them was a "volcanic neck"—a cylindrical cone that had been built up in the vent of an ancient volcano. Here the two "necks" had stood, century after century, wearing slowly away. The Icelanders' name for them was *Lóndrangar*—the Lón Rock Pinnacles.

We drove the truck fairly close to the pinnacles, finding to our surprise that we could nowhere reach the sea without descending a considerable cliff. A strong updraft along the whole cliff front seemed to attract the birds, notably the fulmars. So frequently did they hang in air almost touching the cliff top with their wing tips that I was sorely tempted to crawl out onto a jutting rock and try snatching at them.

About a quarter of a mile east of the Lóndrangar a smooth-topped ridge named Svalthúfa ended abruptly in cliffs overhanging the sea. Much of the cave thus formed was high-ceilinged and shallow, but down near water level, not clearly visible, dark and mysterious looking, a real cave led back into the rock. The Icelanders called the cliffs Thúfubjörg.

This dark cave, the overhanging cliffs above it, and a jagged islet out a rod or so from shore were fairly alive with birds.

Dozing kittiwakes so covered the islet that it was almost snow white. Ledges so narrow that we would never have been aware of them had not the birds been there were lined with common murres. Throngs of murres hid the walls of the dark cave, too, as far back as the eye could see. The clamor that issued from the cave was a loud, rhythmic, gargling bellow—the food cry of hungry young murres. When we threw a pebble down onto the rocks, most of the kittiwakes flew. Unlike the fulmars, they kept away from the cliffs, almost never riding the updraft. Especially interesting to watch were certain adult murres which were not bringing food to the cave. These idlers shot down from the high ledges at breath-taking speed, catching themselves not far above water level, or came in from the sea, rose in a sweeping upcurve, and came to rest with scarcely a flutter. Whole rows of murres looked as if they were standing on nothing at all.

After watching the colony for half an hour, we decided that the murres were the most numerous of the several species. Kittiwakes were common, but we were not sure that they were nesting. Puffins seemed to be nesting not about the cave but in turfy places on the Lóndrangar. We saw fulmars flying to and from the cliffs. Black guillemots were not very common. We did not see a single shag.

Two new birds for our list were the razor-billed auk and the Brünnich's murre or thick-billed guillemot. Neither of these was common, but both apparently were nesting. Occasionally a razor-bill came close to the cliff top, rising confidently on the updraft, giving us a fine look at the narrow white tipping of the secondaries.

While the Pettingills were taking photographs, I found a comfortable spot between the Lóndrangar and spent an hour watching the comings and goings of the hundreds of birds. I shall never forget the ease with which a Brünnich's murre dropped from its nesting ledge about two hundred feet above me, wings spread but quivering rather than beating, until, perhaps thirty feet above the water, it leveled off. Even more impressive was the grace and precision with which it swung up to the ledge when returning with food. Often it came in low, but once the climb started, there was no slowing down, no change in wingbeats, no deviation from course until the ledge was reached.

I have a confession to make to the Pettingills. So comfortable was my sunny, out-of-the-wind observation spot that I slept soundly for a while. When I wakened, the first thing I saw was a row of puffins looking down at me.

Finding the red-throated divers was an interesting experience. We had been told just how to reach the pond and felt sure we had found it, although when we walked around it we saw no divers. Then, recalling how secretive these large birds can be, we looked again in a narrow patch of sedge along a stretch of shore within only a few yards of the parked truck. There, sure enough, was the nest with its one egg. We climbed into the truck and waited. Finally a diver appeared, head low, snaking along partly hidden by the sedge.

While we were watching, a car drove up and a tall man got out. We could tell from the looks he directed toward the sedge that he knew where the loon's nest was. Off came his shoes and socks and in he waded for a closer look at the egg. He was an artist from Reykjavík, a tall, athletic-looking man who gave me his name and the address of his studio. I somehow misplaced these and never looked him up, though I fully intended to.

That night we camped out high on a slope near an ice-cold rushing stream. The wind was sharp, but the Pettingills found a sheltered spot for their tent and I slept in the truck. Before I turned in, I looked up the mountain which towered above us. At the tip of one of those long tongues of green that reached up into the cliffs was a ewe and her two tiny lambs.

In Reykjavík once more, we discussed plans with Finnur Gudmundsson, decided against immediate departure for the Vestmannaeyjar, rejoiced over an item in the mail—a package of corn meal from the United States—and had dinner together quietly at Gildaskálinn. I never gave the Pettingills all of my reasons for liking that restaurant so much. I had, of course, had my first meal in Iceland there; the Pettingills and I had eaten there many times because the waitresses were pleasant and the food good; but my own private liking for the spot stemmed partly from realization that the windows looked out on Adalstraeti, a street believed to be the oldest in Reykjavík. If my conversation ever faltered there, if my gaze ever seemed to linger dreamily on what was half-visible through the clean white window curtains, it was because I was thinking of those who might have been there a thousand years before me. The little book had read, "On the other hand, it may be said that one of the main streets of the town today, Adalstraeti, has developed out of the old track up from the sea to the farm of the first settler—and is thus a street which is a thousand years old." That first settler had been Ingólfur Arnarson. He and his wife, Hallveig Fródadóttir, had come over from Norway. The two of them might have walked together along "the old track up from the sea" many times. Ingólfur and Hallveig: beautiful names these, names worth remembering, whether I pronounced them correctly or not.

Ingólfur and Hallveig crossed my mind more than once the following day during our brief visit to Thingvellir, the Thing Plains, at the head of the big shining lake called Thingvallavatn.

The Thing Plains and the rift known as Almannagjá, which extends for about ten kilometers to the northward of the plains, are enclosed by walls of lava up to one hundred feet high on the west side and about forty-five feet high on the east side. If the traveler approaches from the north, he descends gradually to the level of the plains, but if he approaches, as we did, from the west, he drops through the lava wall, crosses the River Öxará, sees and hears the great cataract Öxarárfoss, and looks down on the famed Drekkingarhylur, or Drowning Pool—just below the bridge to his right—all in one breath.

The plains were beautiful, the well-kept shrines impressive, the bronze tablets, with their record of high deeds done, awe-inspiring. Legend has it that in Drekkingarhylur criminals were drowned.

I did my best to find birds along the rushing river between the bridge and the great fall. The walking was not easy. At every turn I hoped to see a harlequin duck or a merlin. I hardly saw a bird.

But when I returned to the bridge and followed with my eye the swift water below the Drowning Pool, my pulse quickened. In a shallow riffle close to the farther shore, and moving downcurrent rapidly, was a hen harlequin. At first I thought she had chicks with her, but I soon convinced myself that she was alone. Resigning myself to what I knew

164 / *Drekkingarhylur—The Drowning Pool*

might prove to be a long wait, I decided to follow her about until she went to her nest.

I watched her almost an hour. She did not go to a nest. Not the slightest move did she make toward leaving this stretch of stream. She continued to feed in swift water, moving slowly upcurrent close to the bottom. Completely submerged, she nibbled at the rocks. Probably she was finding the larvae of simuliid flies or some other form of animal life that lived in rapidly moving water. Occasionally she rode downstream on the surface to a quiet pool; but most of the time she was on the go, diving, bobbing up for air and a quick look-around, diving again, full of energy, voracious. It was wonderful being able to watch her. The water was clear and shallow, my glass a good one.

All of this was within a stone's throw of the Drowning Pool, a historic spot concerning which I asked my friend Finnur certain questions. His reply included the following: ". . . unfaithful wives were put into a sack and drowned in this pool during the session of the ancient parliament. Male criminals were always executed in a more noble way (beheaded)."

The last sentence furnishes us with an excellent example of what I like to call dramatic punctuation. The first parenthesis has the sound of a falling axe, the second of a heavy object rolling.

XXIII

Climb to the Top of Hellisey

THE VESTMANNAEYJAR (Vestmann or Westmann Islands of most maps) are a cluster of small islands not far off the coast of south central Iceland. They are about 110 kilometers southeast of Reykjavík. On the largest of the group, Heimaey (Home Island), is the only town of the archipelago, Vestmannaeyjar. The Vestmannaeyjar are justly famous for their bird life. On the islets of Hellisey and Ellidaey, whose names continue to embarrass the tip of my tongue, great numbers of sea birds breed. On the steep-sided, towering Hellisey (pronounced *Héd-li-say*), gannets, fulmars, common murres, and kittiwake gulls nest on cliffs accessible only with ropes, while four other species of gulls—the great black-back, lesser black-back, glaucous, and herring—and the puffin nest on the very top. On the much less formidable Ellidaey (pronounced *Éd-li-dthay*) thousands of puffins are caught year after year in hand-operated nets which are something like butterfly nets on a grand scale. To the ornithologist, Ellidaey is of special interest for the Manx shearwater and two species of Mother Carey's chickens—the Leach's petrel and storm petrel—nest there, the shearwater and the Leach's petrel in burrows in the turf, the storm petrel in crevices in the rock. On the tiny islet called Fuglasker or Geirfuglasker, a rock off by itself, the great auk lived, and may even have bred, two hundred years ago. Eggert Ölafsson, an Icelander who studied at the University of Copenhagen and who traveled about Iceland from 1752 to 1757, reported that *Geirfugl* or Garefowl inhabited one islet of the Vestmannaeyjar. This Fuglasker was the islet to which he referred.

The Geirfuglasker widely known to have been inhabited by the great auk were not, however, part of the Vestmannaeyjar. They were reeflike rocks, or skerries, fifteen to twenty miles off Reykjanes, the peninsula forming the southwestern corner of Iceland, and they disappeared beneath the sea during a seismic cataclysm in 1830. These Geirfuglasker were near Eldey Rock (pronounced *Él-dthay*), famous as the spot on which the last great auk specimens known to science were obtained. A pair of the big flightless birds were taken there during the first week of June, 1844. Eldey is inhabited today by one of the largest colonies of gannets in the world.

Sewall discussed with Finnur Gudmundsson the possibility of a special junket to Eldey for a look at the gannets. A greatly enlarged photograph of the colony, a framed picture hanging in Finnur's office, was enough to rouse the interest of anyone, for the thousands of gannets visible there were so astonishingly equidistant from each other that the general effect was that of row upon row of big white flowers in a gigantic rock garden. Finnur informed us that a flight to Eldey was out of the question for pilots were in mortal fear of colliding with one of the great birds. A gannet's wing spread is something like six feet.

As for the Vestmannaeyjar, the Pettingills and I had many times discussed what we might hope to accomplish by a quick trip to them. In good weather we could fly there and back without great trouble or expense, but when the wind rose or the fog closed in, flights were cancelled and we might be stuck there for days during which photography would be impossible. I must confess that I had a special reason for wanting to visit the archipelago: I wanted to dig out and hold in my hands a live Mother Carey's chicken.

The weather being good, we boarded a Vestmannaeyjar-bound plane at eight o'clock Tuesday evening, July 15. Every seat was filled. Next to me sat a young Icelander, a seaman named Einar Kristinsson, who told me he was on his way to Russia. His ship, now anchored in the Vestmannaeyjar and loaded with fish, would probably depart that very night. Einar spoke English well, and for some reason I was fascinated by his enthusiasm for Leningrad. I didn't ask if he was a Communist or what he thought of Communism. I recalled that I had seen Communist newspapers morning after morning in "my" restaurant back on Laekjargata. I had heard a great deal about the Communist leanings of Iceland's great writer, Halldór Laxness, about the Communist influence everywhere, and so on. Being a good American, I hated Communism and everything about it; but there was something refreshing, something downright refreshing, about listening to a likable person who without hesitation praised something Russian. "The trees, the parks, the big buildings—oh, you should see them!" said Einar, delighted because he could give me firsthand information about a part of the world I had never seen. "They are so beautiful. And the people are fine, very fine."

My companion probably had no idea why I was so much interested in what he said about Russia. He knew I was bound for the Vestmannaeyjar, and he naturally assumed that, for the moment at least, I was more interested in them than in anything else. So he proceeded to point out the several islands as they came into view and to tell me of his experiences thereabouts. As I followed his pointing finger and listened to his words, I could not put Russia from my mind. I had heard that three-fourths of Iceland's fish went to Russia, that some went to Nigeria, and that almost none went to the United States. All at once it became apparent to me why relationships between Russia and Iceland were not strained. Russia had no air base on Iceland. Russia bought a great deal of Iceland fish. Many an Icelander who had never visited America had seen a good deal of Russia. "What," I kept asking myself, "has my country been doing to sell itself to Iceland?" "Not much" seemed to be the answer. Here was a young Icelander who, had he seen America, had he become acquainted with Americans, might be loving my country too. Einar's ideas of America may well have come largely from gaudy movie advertisements bearing such words as *Stupendous! With a cast of thousands!*

I did my best to learn from Einar where he would be later that evening, for I wanted to talk further with him; but after we landed, our paths seemed to lead in wholly different directions and I have never set eyes on him since that day, though I have received good letters and Christmas cards from him. His 1959 Christmas card shows several of Iceland's beautiful waterfalls. His message reads—and I treasure every word—"I wich you a Merry Chrystmas and Happy New Year. Yours friendly. Einar Kristinsson."

We were met by a handsome young Lutheran clergyman, the Reverend Jóhann Hlídar, who was courteous, even courtly, who helped us with our luggage, and who escorted us to the Hotel HB, where rooms had been reserved for us. Once we had ensconced ourselves, we went to Rev. Hlídar's house, where, presently, we were joined by an open-faced, athletic-looking young man who was to be our guide. This man, whose nickname sounded like Polly, was Páll Steingrímsson. The accent on the *a* in Páll demanded a pronunciation almost the equivalent of Powell, so Palli, the affectionate diminutive of Páll, became *Powelly* or *Polly*.

In the comfortable and spacious living room Palli astounded us with his knowledge of birds. He even knew their scientific names. Yes, we were told, a boat and crew were ready to take us to Hellisey on the morrow. The boat would stand by while we were on the island: that was the rule whenever Hellisey was concerned. The shores were very steep, so landing was difficult; the weather might turn bad within an hour or so; it might be necessary to leave in a hurry to avoid being stranded. Parties had been stranded there for weeks. We had not thus far experienced any truly vile weather anywhere in Iceland, but we had experienced weather enough to set our imaginations romping. We were more than willing to have the boat stand by; we would gladly fit into any accepted plan. Rev. Hlídar and Palli walked with us back to the hotel. On our way we passed the centuries-old church in which our friend preached.

170 / *Climb to the Top of Hellisey*

A great truck came early for us and our gear, and we were driven to the dock. Our boat, appropriately called the *Lundi*, was ready, but departure was delayed long enough for us to have a look at a boatful of pink lobsters, fresh from the sea. Some of the lobsters, we were told, probably would go to America. I could not help wondering why a market for this particular item had developed when none had developed for fish. The lobsters were not nearly as large as the Maine and Labrador lobsters with which I was familiar, and their front claws were surprisingly slender.

To our delight we learned that Rev. Hlídar and a banker friend of his, a man named Jóhannes Tómasson, were to be part of our little expedition. The boat had a crew of three, all of them seasoned sailors and very fit looking. The morning was fine, there was little wind, and everyone felt we were to have a good day. Palli pointed to the steep slopes just west of town, telling us of the early days when, attacked by pirates, the islanders had sought refuge by climbing the great hill. Some had escaped, but many had died. Up those same slopes our friend Rosario Mazzeo, the famous first violinist of the Boston Symphony, had climbed when he had visited Vestmannaeyjar within the past few years.

The *Lundi*, a well-built craft with stout heart, carried us as directly as possible to Hellisey. Since the weather was fine, the thing to do was travel fast, finish the photographic work promptly, and get off the island while the getting was good. Oh, the cliffs we skirted, the weird caves we passed! Here and there, above us at the edge of the cliff, stood a neat white cross. Every such cross meant that a man had fallen to his death while gathering eggs on the cliff below.

Hellisey seemed to be the highest, the least negotiable

island in sight. Approaching, as we did, from the north, we could see nothing but sheer cliffs hundreds of feet high; on the south side, however, a thin ridge rose like a jagged stone knife out of the sea. Here we were obviously to land. I wondered how we were ever to get ourselves, to say nothing of thirteen pieces of luggage, up the rocks. Presently, below the dark, wet, seaweed-covered tidal zone, on a narrow strip of black beach, we disembarked. The superintendent of the island, hard-bitten of visage and built like a rock, had come down to meet us. With the help of stout ropes we climbed past the seaweed to something like firm footing. How often had I seen seaweed of this sort—on the Labrador, at Frobisher Bay, at Coral Harbor on Southampton Island, even out on the Aleutians! Had the sea been anything but calm we would never have made it. It occurred to me that the whole operation might have been easier had the tide been in, but I made no comment.

Landing was the merest beginning. Guided by the superintendent who seemed to know, quite literally, every blessed step of the way, we made the ascent. There were times when I wondered whether I should try to go farther. I shuddered at the thought of slipping or spraining an ankle, of thus holding things up. I was not limping much, but an occasional pain in my right hip reminded me to be careful.

Finally, after half an hour of climbing, some of it almost on hands and knees, we reached the lowest part of the island's top, a grassy slope protected from the wind. Resting, we looked down on the tiny *Lundi*, then at the rocks up which we had come. The gentlest slopes immediately about us were steep enough, but they seemed positively flat in comparison with those we had just ascended, and the softness of the turf was comforting. The grass continued to the westernmost edge of the island; beyond that was a sheer drop to the sea, an incredible, breath-taking drop of perhaps a thousand feet that made us want to sink to our knees, to hug the rock, to clutch something solid with our hands. On the cliff face were myriads of birds, most of them common murres.

For the men of the *Lundi* and the superintendent of the island there was nothing out of the ordinary about any of this unless it was that they had seen with their own eyes the slender, the not particularly athletic-looking Eleanor Pettingill taking it all in her stride. Not once had she slipped, groaned, or so much as broken a fingernail. I can't help thinking that they were impressed by her performance. Most assuredly I was!

Now were we for the first time to see puffin nets in use. A puffin net or *háfur* (pronounced *hów-foor*) is a stout, slender, tapering wooden pole about eighteen feet long with a tough net, held by the central shaft and by two four-foot supporting prongs, at the pointed end. The catcher, net on the ground beside him, waits at a point past which puffins regularly fly. The best spots are those at which the birds, after flying up a slope out of the wind, suddenly meet the blast and for an instant pause. If the bird is low enough, as it often is, the catcher can raise the net swiftly and catch the bird. Oh, it is a sight to see—the catcher lying in wait, the steady stream of birds coming, coming, coming, the bird that is obviously headed in just the right direction, then that bird's pause, its slight but fatal hesitation, and the swift, sure upswing of the net. The poor bird, entangled in the meshes, bites, flutters, kicks, and growls, but to no avail. The catcher pulls the net back swiftly, hand over hand, deftly extricates the puffin, breaks its neck with a quick pull, returns the net to its position, and is ready for the next bird. On a single good day, when the wind is just right and the birds continue to circle the island, a man in a good position may catch up to five or six hundred puffins.

Palli had his heart set on teaching me how to catch a puffin, so off I went with him to a little ridge he knew about. We sat not far apart, with the long-handled net lying downslope so that Palli could whisk it upward when a puffin came by. The birds were not numerous, nor did my mentor catch a bird with every try, but he caught several, and the handsomest of these, a fine male, he insisted that I keep for my collection.

At length I tried the net myself. First I went through all the motions of lying in wait, of lifting the net swiftly to see how much strength was required, of keeping my feet securely braced. I was determined to avoid catastrophe. The thought of snapping the long handle with too sudden an upthrust, or of pitching down the slope in a series of somersaults, almost made my hair stand on end. Dry runs over, I waited for a puffin. On it came. The worst sort of greenhorn at all this, I lifted the net far too soon, and the puffin veered gracefully off. Then I waited too long, and the puffin shot past so close that I could have touched it with my hand. With the twelfth try I touched a wing tip and made the bird growl a little. This was something like drawing blood, but I continued to miss each and every bird. My chief difficulty was that I was not putting my heart into it. The moves I made were calculated not so much to catch a puffin as to keep net and netter intact. This was no way to catch anything! However mortified Palli may have been over my failure, he smiled indulgently, assuring me that "lots of times" even good puffin catchers miss the birds.

As I made my way back to the little tool shed, a superintendent's headquarters of sorts, I must have been feeling rather predatory. In any event, as I climbed a big gash in the rock, planning thus to reach a more level stretch of turf, I frightened a fulmar from its egg and the beautiful bird, heading directly for the sea, flew so close that with only a little jump I caught it by one wing. It vomited, struggled violently, and bit my hands, but I held it firmly. This specimen I needed, for I had no adult fulmar in my collection; so realizing that it had only an egg, that killing it would not mean the starvation of a chick, I cut off its oxygen supply by squeezing it hard under the wings. It was a lovely creature—creamy-white on the head, neck, and under parts, light gray on the back and upper surface of the wings. This was the bird the Icelanders called the *fyll* (pronounced *fée-dle*).

Meanwhile Sewall, enamored of the gannets, had climbed to the highest part of the island. He and his camera were now perched on a knob from which he could look down on a broad ledgeful of gannets and their young. The chicks were of various ages. Some which looked every bit as heavy as their parents were covered with thick, snow-white down and were pudgy and helpless beyond belief. Palli and I joined the photographer. Palli, sure-footed as a chamois, jumped to the gannet's ledge as unconcernedly as if he had been stepping from a curbstone to the street, and picked one of the biggest of the babies up. The high-pitched yapping was hideous and the thrusts of the bill vicious, but the fluffy armful was only a baby, and Palli knew just how to handle it.

Not far from the nesting ledge was a point of rock near

which the old gannets, supported by the powerful updraft as they flew in, hung on all but motionless wings for moments at a stretch. Palli and I watched the great birds, fascinated by their clean-cut beauty and by their mastery of the air. Their wings curled upward at the very tips, but there was no slotting of the outermost three, four, or five primary feathers comparable to that in an eagle's or condor's wings. The wedge-shaped tail veered this way and that, keeping the heavy body headed straight toward the nesting ledge. If the tail did not accomplish quickly enough the task of steering, out went one great foot or the other. Each bird watched us with its big, light-yellow eye. Always, it seemed to me, the pupil of this eye was contracted to its smallest possible size, a tiny pinpoint of black.

Palli and I, schoolboys or hoodlums at heart, found ourselves flicking pebbles at the big birds. We had not the slightest desire to kill or hurt them, but there they were, only a few feet away, daring us to ruffle their imperturbability. I shall not say how many pebbles we threw, nor shall I discuss the size of the pebbles. Once or twice we struck a wing feather, and such forthright hits did fluster the birds a bit. Charmed lives they led, those *súlur* of the Icelanders, and indescribably lovely they were as they hung mid-air with the wrinkled gray-blue of the sea behind and below them.

We ate our lunch in a windless spot near the superintendent's tool shed. The puffin netters reported that they had not caught many birds. When I had finished eating, I skinned out the fulmar specimen, using my pocket knife. To keep my fingers dry I needed cornmeal. One of the men of the *Lundi* found some fine dust for me under a loose rock. Fortunately the fulmar was not very fat and, since it had not been shot, there was not a trace of blood on its plumage.

On our way down to the *Lundi* we were obliged to climb around some big rocks close to the island's west face. Here, peeking through a narrow defile, we saw almost within touching distance a stately row of common murres. They stood upright on a narrow shelf, each only a few inches from its neighbors. They eyed us seemingly without alarm, opening their yellow-lined beaks wide as they shrieked a welcome to, and made room for, newcomers. We gathered that this was not a nesting ledge, for we could see neither eggs nor chicks there; but on ledges not far away half-grown chicks were crowding each other savagely, bellowing for food whenever an old bird flew past or returned to their midst. Among the dozen or so adults that we could see clearly were several "ringed" individuals—birds with a narrow white line encircling and leading back from each eye. Never before had I seen so many murres of this "ringed" color phase in one place at one time.

As we picked our way down to the point of embarkation, we realized more fully than we had during our ascent how steep the slope was. It is doubtful that we could have made the last twenty feet or so without the help of ropes. Be this as it may, I recall the stab of fear I felt on seeing Eleanor, well below and ahead of me, suddenly swinging in mid-air, not in danger actually, for the superintendent, who was swinging too, had one arm tightly about her. They were on the last lap of the descent.

I had planned to skin the puffin and finish the fulmar on the boat trip back, but the cliffs and caves and colonies of

Climb to the Top of Hellisey / 177

birds were so awe-inspiring that I could not take my eyes from them. To our surprise we rounded the west side of Heimaey, thus varying our course.

The wind-whipped sea was choppy enough to make us appreciate the snugness of the harbor. Rev. Hlídar had dinner with us at the hotel. I managed to prepare the fulmar and puffin specimens before the evening was over, but the notes that went into my log were sketchy and all but illegible. As I finished my work I heard the squeals of little boys and girls at play off to the west of town. Curious because the children seemed to be having such an extra good time of it, I looked from the window in the fading light, using my binocular. There they were—lined up on ledges not far above the bases of the cliffs, swinging on long ropes from one ledge to another. Joyful they were to the point of hilarity. I was tired, more than ready to call it a day. Not so the kiddies. I could hear their shrill laughter as I dropped off to sleep.

XXIV

Puffin Catching

BREAKFAST, at a reasonable hour the following morning, was a meal the Pettingills and I have often discussed. We had made clear to the management that we expected the meal to be a full one, not just a snack, the point being that we would be afield and working hard all day if the good weather held. Eggs had been specified, bacon mentioned. But the sight of that table, fully set with all we had ordered plus what the management had intended to give us in the first place, was beyond belief. There was a huge platter of fried eggs, cold, sunny-side up; sliced hard-boiled eggs; light bread and dark; sardines; herrings in wine sauce; cornflakes; sliced cheese; tomatoes; cucumbers (rinds on, sliced thin, delicious!); cold roast beef; cold breaded lamb; pickles; beets; jelly; butter and coffee. It was a meal to discuss—and to demolish. All three of us had eaten Continental breakfasts. There was nothing Continental about this one; this one gloried in its insularity; this one, like the cows back at Bessa-stadir, was *Icelandic*.

Off we set for Ellidaey, excited but hardly in a dither, for this time we knew our boat and crew, the weather was good and, besides, the island was not far away. Landing was easy and carrying our gear up to the little building that we dubbed "The Puffin Catchers' Club" was not much of a job. The slopes were gentle, the whole of the interior was turfy, and sheltered places were thickly covered with grass.

Many sheep lived on the island. Seeing the animals did not surprise us, but it did remind us that we had not seen any on Hellisey. As we watched a ewe and her lambs on a green patch far above us, we noted a little enclosure, a sort of corral, just above the edge of a cliff. So roused was our curiosity by this seemingly out-of-place structure that we asked about it. "Oh, that is for the sheep," was the reply. "In winter they can't get down by themselves, so they go into that pen and we let them down with ropes."

At "the Club" were were almost awed by the amenities. The furnishings of the one room were not elegant, but we sat in a cozy ring at the big table while rawboned men quietly made coffee, passed cups around, and handed out snow-white napkins. Not all of our companions spoke English, but every one of them was courteous and friendly, and the coffee was delicious. We were assured that the wind was right for puffin catching and that many Mother Carey's chickens and shearwaters were nesting on the island. We were also told that since it was daytime we would have to dig the petrels and shearwaters out if we expected to see them. If we wanted to observe them in action, if we wanted to hear their cries and feel the wind from their wings, we would have to visit Ellidaey after dark, for it was only then that these far-wandering birds returned from the sea to their burrows.

I wish I had written down the name of the man who volunteered to find me a *stóra saesvala*, a Leach's petrel. He had seen one of the birds at the entrance to its burrow an evening or so before, so he felt sure he could obtain one for me. He picked up a spade, and, walking rapidly, led me upslope to the very edge of the island. The cliff below us was neither as high nor as precipitous as those on Hellisey, but the look I had at the crawling sea, far below us, thrilled me through and through. Where the turf met the rock at the cliff's very brink there were scattered holes—entrances to burrows. These had been dug by the Leach's petrels, the species that had laid its eggs in early June. The storm petrel, a smaller species with squarish rather than forked tail, was a late nester by comparison. Many storm petrels laid their eggs in early July, but egg laying continued until September. The Icelandic name for the storm petrel was *litla saesvala*.

My companion did not dig more than eight or ten chunks of turf away before he found a petrel. There the small bird was, shuffling awkwardly along what was left of its ruined burrow, bewildered, frightened, dazed by the sudden light. My friend sensed how exciting and wonderful all this was to me. He let me pick the bird up—the first living Mother Carey's chicken I had ever held in my hands. How darkly beautiful and how otherworldly it was! I was struck with the shyness, almost the sadness, written on its face; then, remembering how often I had told students of the special smell museum specimens of petrels invariably have, I held the bird to my nose. Sure enough the odor was there, that strange odor that for me had so unfailingly conjured up the vastness of the ocean, the quiet, inexorable strength of waves, the joy and freedom and amazing fortitude of these delicate little walkers-on-the-sea.

With the petrel in my hand I thought back to the summer of 1938 when, returning from Europe on the *City of Baltimore,* I had often watched the tiny black "chickens" feeding about the vessel. How tireless they were! Never did they stop to rest, never did they coast along on set wings for more than a few yards at a stretch. For them life seemed to be an endless fluttering—a fluttering interrupted now and then by a snatching up of food, a swift pattering of webbed feet dropped to full length, a keeping to the deepest parts of the troughs between the waves in rough weather. I remembered especially two petrels, each deep in a trough and separated from the other by the smooth, swiftly running crest of a wave. There they were, the two of them in that vast watery world where there certainly was elbow room, if nothing else; the two birds, each hidden from the other, decided to slip over the wave into the next trough; they headed for each other as if carried on wires that crossed at the wave's crest and . . . collided. I could almost hear the crash. Dazed, the birds floated a second or two before fluttering up and away.

The man with the spade seemed to feel that I should have another specimen, so he started digging. The second burrow was, like the first, far from straight. It led this way and that, never far below the surface, sometimes almost doubling back into itself. There were side burrows, too—false starts perhaps. This time a long stretch of burrow was laid open—a total of perhaps three yards, and I began to suspect that more than one burrow was involved. I noticed that my friend laid each chunk carefully to one side. Not one piece was flung carelessly over the cliff edge. At the end of a burrow we found two petrels together, an adult and a chick, the latter covered with long, shaggy, sooty-gray down, and as helpless a creature as I have ever seen. It could not stand. When it put out a wing it seemed to have no notion as to how to pull that heavy, useless appendage back into place. It was, indeed, a creature of the nether world, of the darkness. Quite possibly it had never before seen the light of day.

The three petrel specimens now in my possession gave me a sensation of completeness, of a rounding-out of life, that I have not often felt. Hundreds of times, yes, hundreds of times in teaching or lecturing, I had made statements about petrels—interesting statements too, most of them based on what someone else had told me, or on what someone else had written. Here I stood on an island called Ellidaey, with a cold wind blowing in straight from the Atlantic, a wind so strong I felt a twinge of fear as I looked over the cliff, with a real Icelander at my side, with a real petrel burrow at my feet, with three live Leach's petrels in a little box in my hand. This was what I had been growing toward; this was the flowering; now I would *know* what I was talking about when I talked about petrels.

Our hunt was not over. Not by any means was it over. The final stage was a gesture of patriotism, of love for the homeland, entirely new to me. With tenderness beyond description this new found friend of mine lifted chunk after chunk of turf in his hands, ascertained how each had been spaded away, and put it back exactly as he had found it. With this I helped him. When we left the spot, there was no way of knowing that the turf had been disturbed—no way except that the entrances to the burrows were now very hard to descry. Thus it was that the Icelanders kept their land, the soil itself, in order. Thus did they prevent the wind and rain from gouging it away. Thus did they preserve the turf in which grew the grass their sheep ate, in which nested that highly prized resource of theirs, the *lundi*, the puffin.

It is a circumstance hardly to be wondered at that I cannot remember what was happening to the Pettingills while I was after petrels. Doubtless they were risking their necks somewhere, taking pictures, for that was their wont. When my companion and I returned to "the Club," we found that almost everyone had departed for the south end of the island —for certain spots at which the puffin netters made their best hauls.

One of the men waiting for us had been chosen to help me find a Manx shearwater. Here again was a bird I had often talked about but never drawn, nor handled in the flesh, nor even seen alive. Two larger shearwaters, the greater and the sooty, I had seen many times along the Labrador; indeed, I might possibly have seen the Manx shearwater more than once during two Atlantic crossings in 1938, but I had never been sure that I was seeing it, so now that I was in a place known to be part of its breeding range I was eager to become acquainted with it.

The grassy slope to which we walked appeared to me to be in no way unusual. The turf was spongy underfoot. The grass grew in bunches, and I noticed very few flowers anywhere. Presently we began to find entrances to burrows— ill-defined openings, partly hidden by vegetation. My companion, who spoke English well, got down on all fours and listened closely at each burrow entrance. "Sometimes you hear the puffin, the *lundi*, making its odd sounds," he said. "The *skrofa*, the shearwater, usually is silent in its burrow, but not the *lundi*."

I listened too, but heard no sounds. There seemed to be no way of telling from the condition of the grass whether entrances had been used or not. Nowhere could we find a dropping of any sort, or evidence that food had been brought. Every entrance seemed to be perfectly clean. My companion, who smoked a pipe, got to work with his spade, and soon great chunks of turf lay alongside an exposed burrow. At the first burrow, the second, the third, we drew a blank. Immediately after excavating a burrow we replaced the turf with care. The burrows led downward a considerable distance, sometimes two feet or more, before leveling off.

At the fourth burrow a puffin flopped out and away just as my friend started to dig. The fifth burrow was empty, as was the sixth. By the time nine burrows had been opened up, the digging was beginning to seem like work. I was disappointed, of course, and also a little surprised, for I had expected every burrow to be occupied.

At the end of the tenth burrow we found our shearwater —a soft, pathetically wobbly chick, about half-grown, but still covered with down. Like the petrel chick it was utterly helpless. It was, I believe, the softest creature I ever handled. It was mouse gray above, creamy white below. The down on its back was much longer than that on its under parts, and less dense. Nowhere could we find either of the parent birds. Almost certainly they were at sea.

Now that we had three petrels and a shearwater, we decided to join the puffin catchers. On our way from "the Club" to the southern edge of the island we passed a little shed near which recently captured puffins were strewn in the grass. A hundred or so birds lay there, ready to be stored in ice.

From a high point on which several sheep grazed my companion led me down a steep declivity toward a spot known to be exceptionally good for catching puffins. Presently I could see well ahead and at slightly lower level, a company of dead puffins, propped up in such a way as to decoy incoming birds. As long as we were in sight, no puffins came close, but the minute we crouched—in holes the puffin netters had used, literally for centuries—the birds began flying past. Soon the nets were doing their work. The wind was just right. One netter had sixty or so birds in the grass back of him. This man was a real expert; he rarely missed.

I noticed that no move was made to catch a bird that was carrying food in its beak. This passing up of parent birds with chicks was a matter neither of accident nor of shallow sentiment. Regulation or no regulation, it was counter to common sense to kill birds that were rearing young. Careful marking of birds had shown Icelanders long since that one-year-old puffins lead an oceanic life, never approaching land, but that two-year-old birds visit the nesting colonies and continue to do so until they themselves start nesting. Most of the birds captured on good puffin days were known to be nonbreeding, immature birds with nothing better to do than circle the island. Breeding birds were nearly always recognizable from the limp, slender fish they held crosswise in the beaks. Thus had come into being the custom of allowing food-carrying birds to fly by unmolested. Thus had come about the annual capture, on Ellidaey alone, of something like thirty thousand plump, full-grown, tasty *nonbreeding* puffins. There is no law preventing an Icelander from catching all that he can catch in a day, or in a season, so long as he passes up the food-carrying birds. For me, a man who had delivered hundreds of talks on the conservation of natural resources in America, a man who had witnessed the final stages of the extermination of the American heath hen, a man who had dreamed of leading his own people to a proper evaluation and use of its wildlife, for me these facts about Iceland's puffin harvest were thrilling. The thing worked: a people *could* eat a fine big cake and have it too!

I wonder what I could have said or done that led my companions to believe that I wanted to learn how to catch puffins. I suppose my friend Palli had told them that I was out to learn every trick of my trade. Be this as it may, the expert netter himself embarrassed me no end by insisting that I take his position and use his net and he nodded so reassuringly that as I stepped into those thousands-of-times-used foot holes I began feeling very professional indeed. I would keep low. I would wait for precisely the right moment. I would not budge until the instant for moving had arrived, then up the net would shoot at exactly the right speed, and the poor puffin would flutter and bite at the net and groan and croak at me just as it would have groaned and croaked at a real puffin netter. The experience on Hellisey had taught me a little. My subconscious had been at work too.

Let no one be bored with details. I have no idea how many times I tried or how many times I missed. What I know is that I netted four puffins, quite by myself, and that one of them I caught (just as it was getting out of range) with a follow-through maneuver which so surprised me that it took my breath and which so delighted the expert that he shouted approval and clapped his hands—plaudits that go down in memory as among the sweetest I ever heard.

At killing my birds I was awkward. The expert had shown me two or three ways of breaking necks, methods that appeared to be simple enough, but every bird I caught was a die-hard. The Pettingills delight to tell of one of my victims which, having had its neck "broken," stood up, contemplated its surroundings with understandable dissatisfaction, and whirred off. I have argued that this bird was not one of my four, but I have never been able to convince the Pettingills.

The expert netter was, I observed, paying special attention to the murres that flew past. A few of these he caught. One of them, a large male of the beautiful "ringed" color phase, he gave me for my collection. It is the only "ringed" murre I have ever handled in the flesh.

Before returning to "the Club," I went to an eminence beyond the spot at which I had caught my puffins, my plan being to help the Pettingills carry back their heavy equipment. From this new position I looked down at the slope on which I had so thoroughly enjoyed myself half an hour before. What I saw was beyond belief. The whole blessed slope, grass, rocks, netters' stations and all, overhung the sea. The shore itself, with its narrow white line of surf, was barely visible back under the jutting promontory. The very look of it all made me dizzy.

I was sorely tempted to spend the night on Ellidaey, for I wanted very much to hear the calls of the shearwaters and petrels as they returned to their burrows, but I felt an obligation to the birds I already had; they were giving their lives in my behalf; I could not fail them. My painting outfit was at the hotel. To sketch the petrels now in my possession would require a careful scheduling of what was left of the day. I asked the men at "the Club" to obtain an adult shearwater and a storm petrel for me if they could.

Rev. Hlídar had invited us to dine with him at his home that evening. When we got back to our hotel rooms, I set to work at once on a pencil sketch of the head of the Leach's petrel, doing my best to record the solemn, mysterious, helpless expression that all Mother Carey's chickens seem to wear on their faces. The outlines went down well. The colors I would add in the strong morning light of the morrow.

Dinner was memorable not alone for the excellence of the stewed puffins but also for the vitality and sparkle of the conversation. Palli wanted to know more about American colleges and universities. Our host was deeply interested in philosophy, in world trends, in "universals." My experiences with the Aivilik Eskimos raised question after question about this fine tribe, and, inspired by the obvious sincerity of everyone's interest, I became voluble on a subject very close to my heart—the right of any culture to evolve and flower without the interference of white men. Often the talk dwelt upon religious matters. I was surprised by Sewall's interest in all this. I was touched when I heard him say, afterwards, "It was a wonderful evening, wasn't it?"

The day wound up with a brief visit at Palli's house, where we met his pretty wife Edda and his sweet little daughter Hildur. In one of the basement rooms a young murre was bellowing for food. Palli showed us two mounted birds, a male harlequin duck and a strange common murre, brownish-black all over, a melanistic individual unlike any murre I had ever seen or heard of. The house, made of a mixture of cement (one part), volcanic ash (two parts), and sand and gravel (four parts), Palli had built himself, with the help of some of his friends, at a cost of about 9,700 *krónur* ($255 American money) in wages.

The following day (Friday, July 18) was somewhat tedious for me. I thrilled at the beauty of the morning, the feel of the cool air, the very thought of being in the Vestmannaeyjar. But why be in such a place if one could not be out and in it, part of it all? It would be a wonderful day for photography. Palli's younger brother, Svavar Steingrímsson, an expert at rope work on the big cliffs, was to give a special exhibition of his prowess. The Pettingills were elated.

My job was catching up on indoor work that had to be done. The petrel drawing was to be finished. Petrel, shearwater, and murre specimens were to be prepared. The murre I planned to draw, for I wanted an authentic record of the way in which those tiny white feathers of the ring and line back of the eye lay in the unskinned bird. To my annoyance I found that I was short on supplies. At the town's only *apótek* (drugstore) I obtained plaster of Paris, borax, and carbon tetrachloride.

The young shearwater gave me more "fat trouble" than any specimen I had ever handled. After killing it, I put it on my fiber suitcase, expecting to skin it shortly. As it lay there, oil ran from its mouth and nostrils all over the suitcase and onto the floor—a veritable pool of the disagreeable stuff. The long soft down was saturated. I thought for a moment that the specimen was ruined, but I knew that carbon tetrachloride was a powerful degreasing agent and I had learned from years of experience not to give up easily. I skinned the bird out, using quantities of dry sand as an absorbent. I scraped the inside of the skin over and over, trying to rid it

LUNDI

Puffin chick taken from burrow on
Melrakkaey or Island of the Fox near Setberg, Iceland,
and painted direct from life July 12, 1958.

LANGVÍA

Adult common murre of the ringed phase
captured on Ellidaey, an islet of the Vestmannaeyjar
off the southern coast of Iceland and painted July 18, 1958.

of fat. Realizing that the day was being wasted by all this hack work, I stuffed the far from finished skin crudely, and set it to one side.

The murre drawing turned out well, except that it was a trifle oversize. Preparing the skin was not difficult as the bird was not very fat.

At eight o'clock that evening we boarded the plane for Reykjavík. Our faithful friends were there to see us off. Cloud conditions forced us to fly very low. Below us spread broad valleys strewn with braided rivers. Occasionally we saw a great skua or whooper swan.

Most of one more day I spent scraping fat from the skin of that half-grown shearwater. I used up most of my corn meal supply, all of the carbon tetrachloride, most of the plaster of Paris. Slowly fluffiness returned to the down and hope to the dejected preparator. I could not blow and pound the plaster from the plumage in the apartment so took the specimen out of doors for this part of the operation. The children of the neighborhood became interested and gathered in a lively flock whenever I appeared. The chatter and questioning (in a language I could not understand) would have got out of hand had it not been for a fine lad perhaps fourteen years old, slightly taller than the others, who lined them up and gave them a lecture on the proprieties. I could not understand a word he spoke, but the gist of what he had to say was unmistakable and its effect on his hearers was remarkable. When, from that moment, a peep one shade too loud sounded, up went a dozen fingers to a dozen sets of lips. The Pettingills and I had long since agreed that Iceland's children were the most beautiful we had ever seen. When I looked at those bright faces about me, every one of them fairly bursting with interest and energy, I wanted to put on a special show for them, to skin a big bird out from start to finish right in front of them.

The mallard ducks at Reykjavík were now almost wholly in eclipse plumage. A few hens still were accompanied by chicks, but the drakes all looked oddly like the species we called the black duck in America, and I could not help noticing how beautiful they were. I had fallen into the habit of thinking of the eclipse plumage as incomplete, dull, even dowdy. These mallard drakes were not by any means as gorgeous as they had been a few weeks back when their heads were shining green and their collars clean and white, but now that the quiet-toned summer plumage was complete they were as elegant as ever and as neat as pins. I was so much interested in this female-like "winter" plumage, worn so unseasonably, that I could hardly take my eyes from the birds. I watched them by the hour, wishing for the opportunity to study them at closer range, to photograph them in color, to prepare a fine series of skins. By July 20 hardly a drake of the great flock had a green feather left in its head.

XXV

A Drive Into the Sea

ON SUNDAY, JULY 20, I mentioned to Árni Waag that I had not yet found an arctic skua nest. I was especially interested in chicks of this species, for I wondered if they came in two color phases, as did the adults. I had never visited a region in which there were so many wholly dark adult birds. The color-phase phenomenon puzzled me the more since I had observed a great deal of variation among arctic tern chicks, a species whose adult plumage was not in the least two-phased. Some newly hatched arctic terns were brown, others gray, and there seemed to be every possible variation between the two extremes.

Árni promptly suggested that we visit the nest he had shown the Pettingills while I was recovering from my fall into the drainage ditch. The adult birds at this nest had both been dark all over. He had last seen the two eggs on June 15. He did not know exactly when either egg had been laid, but since the incubation period was known to be about twenty-eight days, we were justified in believing that both chicks would have hatched by this time. I knew from experience in Arctic America that the chicks might not remain long in the nest itself but they would not be likely to wander far during the fledging period.

Árni's little son Hjálmar climbed into "Big Blue" with us, and the three of us headed southward out of Reykjavík. Sudurlandsvegur, the much used thoroughfare that we followed, was terribly dusty. The summer was the driest within the memory of all the Icelanders we knew. The vegetation near the highway was gray with dust—with fine volcanic ash, to be exact. Many lowlands that were normally marshy were dry as a bone. Arriving at the little valley in which the skua chicks should have been, we found family parties of whimbrels and golden plovers, and finally the two parent skuas, which feigned injury repeatedly but did not disclose the whereabouts of their progeny.

A trifle discouraged by this failure, as well as by the dustiness, which was especially bad just outside the city, we returned to find Finnur Gudmundsson organizing a trip for Sewall, himself, and me to Vík, a small but important village on the south coast of Iceland. We would be gone only a day or so. We would travel in Finnur's jeep, which could be closed in tight to keep out the dust. Near Vík we would see the great skua—a species I was especially eager to observe.

I wondered what gear to pack. I decided against item after item on the grounds that what we had on our backs would probably be sufficient clothing for two or three days' needs. My painting outfit I took, every bit of it, and a small taxidermic kit. That was about all. We left early in the afternoon on July 21.

Our first major stop was at the town of Hveragerdi. Here there was a big outdoor swimming pool and a veritable galaxy of hothouses in which tomatoes, cucumbers, carrots, parsley, roses, chrysanthemums, grapes, and bananas were growing. The heat inside the houses was almost more than I could bear, but the plants seemed to thrive in it. There was something inspiring about this use the Icelanders were making of their steam. They were growing vegetables and fruits that could not possibly have been grown outdoors, and they were doing it by harnessing a force that might—the thought crossed my mind with the swiftness of a falcon's stoop—blow them to kingdom come. I recalled Robert Louis Stevenson's glorious essay, *"Aes Triplex,"* especially the part about the carefree happiness of people living in the very shadow of Vesuvius, people who might well have been miserable imagining what could happen to them in case of an eruption, but who sang, danced, and lived joyously instead. Here was no smoldering Vesuvius, to be sure; but here was Hekla, a Hekla that only a few years before had devastated a wide area. And here were all these greenhouses, with their tomatoes turning a happy red, and their insolent roses, as pretty as any I had ever seen!

Ever since arriving in Iceland we had been eating Iceland-grown tomatoes and had commented repeatedly on their excellent flavor. The cucumbers were so tender that we relished every bit of them, rind and all. We were informed that one of the hothouses at Hveragerdi had produced tomatoes worth 200,000 *krónur* in one summer. The growing season lasted about nine months; during the three months of the darkest part of winter there was not enough sunlight to keep the plants alive.

I was especially interested in the grapes, big bunches of which were hanging from the vines. Surprised and amused, I watched an attendant snipping off grapes with small scissors, not bunch by bunch but grape by grape, removing the nearly ripe ones without injuring the others, placing these firm reddish ones in little cellophane sacks for sale in the markets.

The grape snipper could see that I was interested in what he was going. I told him that I was from Oklahoma and that I had never been in Iceland before. Curious about the grapes, which I could see were neither Concords nor Niagaras, and which were not at all like Malagas, I asked him what kind they were. Before he answered, he looked at me slyly, with an appraising twinkle in his eye, as if wondering whether an average American might be expected to know as much about American literature as an average Icelander did about Icelandic. "One of our names for them"—he gave a low chuckle—"is John Steinbeck. How is that for a name?" The laughter that followed this sally must have been as hearty as any the grapes had heard all summer.

Our journey eastward was a succession of sweeping vistas and heart-warming experiences. There was Hekla—majestic, awesome, a serene goddess contemplating a domain she has brought almost to ruin. There were rivers, many of them broad, shallow, heavily silt-laden. One of them smelled strongly of sulphur. Another looked like flowing mud. While flying back from the Vestmannaeyjar, we had looked down on these very streams, some of which were famous for their salmon.

For an hour or so we stopped at a farm where the whole family was haying. What a picture it was—the gaudy new machinery moving swiftly about, some of it, off in the distance, cutting; some raking; some kicking the partly dried swaths about as if in pure frolic! I was amused by the obvious enjoyment a teen-age lad was having backing his implement about, though why he was backing it was beyond me. Several women were using hand rakes. Little boys and girls were helping as best they could. No one was merely observing. Every blessed person was doing something—the one exception being a baby in a new perambulator parked by the fence. The people must have realized they were being photographed, but their behavior was not in the least self-conscious. Used to being busy, they merely speeded things up a bit.

The names on the signposts continued to fascinate Sewall and me. At one forking of the highway, where we had stopped to look around, the long place names so challenged us that we asked Finnur for a moment in which to practice before giving him our pronunciation. We mumbled to ourselves, remembering that the first syllable, no matter how long the word, always got the accent, then spoke the words aloud. "Splendid! Better than the Icelanders could do!" said Finnur. This was the overstatement, the big white lie, of the summer.

We reached Vík late, but not too late for a drive farther eastward through the pleasant evening air. Finnur wanted us to have a glimpse of the country in which the great skua lived and of a certain isolated bluff, known as Hjörleifshöfdi, on whose crags a large fulmar colony nested. The road led along the north edge of Mýrdalssandur, the broad coastal plain. To our left the land rose sharply to a considerable height. The great skua country was this Mýrdalssandur, a many-square-miles area laid waste by volcanic action, flat, covered with dark sand, almost wholly devoid of vegetation. Out in this gray wilderness, which seemed to stretch off endlessly to the south and east, was a steep-sided mountain or hill—in Oklahoma we would have called it a mesa if it had been a bit flatter on top—with extensive patches of green on it. This was Hjörleifshöfdi. Finnur told us that there was a house up there somewhere, with a good road leading to it. Down on the flat he pointed out a little "rescue station," one of several such buildings placed at regular intervals along the whole of this coast, which was notorious for its shipwrecks.

On our way back to Vík, Finnur stopped the jeep, climbed out, and, without a word as to what he intended to do, started rapidly up a steep slope toward a sort of saddle that connected a jutting pinnacle with the big mountain mass just north of us. Let no one call Finnur Gudmundsson a "closet naturalist." The rapidity with which he, for all his more than two hundred pounds, went up that slope had Sewall and me panting before we had climbed ten rods. Birds were about and above us, chiefly puffins, which obviously had burrows in the turf, but also fulmars. On the saddle at last, several hundred feet above the sandy plain, we looked southward toward the sea, westward toward Vík, still farther westward to the great stone arch known as Dyrhólaey or "Door Rock." The grass in which we stood was lush and deep. In sheltered places between great boulders a hardy-looking annual that reminded me of wild parsnip was luxuriant. Thousands of buttercups were blooming on the steep south slope up which we had come. The evening sky made me think not so much of a fine painting as of a familiar old hymn sung quietly.

Most of Vík, a pretty village, was at the level of the plain over which we had just driven, but the church, simple of line, white walled, almost austere, stood on higher ground overlooking the several homes, the hostelry and school. Dinner, at a really late hour, was excellent. I was glad there were no specimens to skin.

I may be pardoned for calling the following day "the day of the great skua." For Sewall the big birds were nothing new; he had seen a closely allied south polar skua thousands of times on the Falklands. But for me the great skua was very special. It was one of the few birds in my life that had managed to stay beyond reach. I had seen it a few times on the Labrador, usually at considerable distance. I had read of its breeding on Lady Franklin Island, but that record had been questioned. Despite the eagerness of American bird students to consider *Catharacta skua* a breeding species of the New World there was no valid record to back up such a concept. When I began laying plans for a summer in Iceland, the great skua was one of the first birds to enter my mind.

Into the great skua habitat we plunged. The redoubtable Finnur, trusting that four-wheel-drive jeep of his, left the road and we roared through the sand. There seemed to be no bad spots to watch for. It was all bad. The sun, the mountains off to the north, the high Hjörleifshöfdi which Finnur had pointed out—these helped us to keep our directions straight, but I had an odd feeling that we were entering a land whose physical laws might be different from those of the world in which I had thus far lived.

Then we began seeing the skuas—big, dark-brown, blunt-looking birds with short tail, broad wings, and heavy beak. Each wing had a whitish spot in it, out toward the tip. A swift changing of course told us that Finnur had seen something. Presently we caught up with a skua chick, and what had been the roar of the jeep became the roar of wings as the adult skuas swooped at us. Finnur wanted the chick for his museum collection—it was much too old for the sort of drawing I wanted—so he handed me his shotgun and I went after the adults. How their attacks unsettled me! They came close, very close at times, but they never struck. I shot at one, and may have touched it, but it flew off strongly, disappearing to the northward. I killed the other bird dead. What a tough, battle-scarred veteran it was!

Not far from where the skua hit the ground we found the wing quills and bones of a fulmar. "Killed by the skuas," explained Finnur. "There are no lemmings anywhere in Iceland and there are no small birds anywhere in this desert country, but the fulmars have to cross the wide plain in reaching their nesting places back in the cliffs and the skuas live on them. The fulmar colonies here are up to fourteen kilometers from the sea. So far as I know, this is the only part of Iceland in which the great skua regularly preys upon adult fulmars."

We saw several pairs of great skuas and found several large chicks, but not until late in the morning did we find a chick young enough for the drawing I needed. We were fortunate to find it so late in the season. It was a droll, dumpy little creature, unable to move very fast and given to stepping on its own toes. Its somewhat plush-like down was a beautiful vinaceous shade of brown. As I picked it up, I felt a rush of wind as one of the old birds barely missed me. The call note of the parent birds was a sullen *heck* or *huck*.

Now that I had a living chick to paint, I was eager to get to work. But Finnur, knowing that an hour more in this desert would help us to remember it more vividly, started driving southward, straight into the sea. "Into the sea" is an exaggeration, of course, but I know no other way of reporting our sensations accurately. The mirage into which we continued to drive was the most completely convincing I have ever seen. Only a few rods ahead of us the water sparkled, water so wet looking, so bright and blue, that it was hard, downright hard, to restrain ourselves from shouting at our driver. Resolutely, almost fiercely, the jeep lunged toward the water, never pausing. When finally we did reach the shore and heard the lapping of the waves, I wondered what new sort of make-believe we were experiencing.

XXVI

At Last—

The Golden Plover Chick

SEWALL WAS A BRICK during all of this skua chasing. The
day was fine, so he must have been itching to get at his
own work, but he uttered not a peep of complaint. Toward
noon we went back to Vík. Finnur decided that the best
workplace for me was at the big school building, now empty.
Finding the key held us up a while, but the entire citizenry
seemed eager to help and it was not long before the heavy
doors were opened.

The room I chose was spacious and well lighted. I set to
work. The chick, though perfectly healthy, seemed to be
incapable of rapid movement and was therefore a good
model. My pencil outline was just about finished when I
realized that the chick and I were not, strictly speaking,
alone. At each of the two big windows was a solid row of
faces. Insatiably curious, the village children had come to
see what was going on. No move that I made was lost to

them. All afternoon, while I was finishing my two drawings and preparing the chick's skin, there were faces at the windows. I did not have time enough for skinning out the adult specimen.

We dined at eight o'clock. The soup was delicious. I could not seem to get enough of it. Finnur and Sewall gave me a complete account of the afternoon's operations. They had secured some excellent footage at Dyrhólaey, and Finnur had shot for me an immature great black-backed gull and a fine black arctic skua, the most perfect specimen of this melanistic color phase that I had ever handled. These specimens had been refrigerated for me.

Breakfast was served late the following morning, so we did not begin our return to Reykjavík until about ten o'clock. The weather was good. We planned to shoot a few birds for my collection and to stop for pictures as Sewall chose. Some distance west of Vík, Finnur took us on another wild dash into the great skua habitat. This time I thought surely we were in for trouble, for some of the terrain was rough and certain flat, low places had a sinister, lying-in-wait appearance that made me think of quicksand; but on we went—downslope, upslope, around rocks, across sand and gravel beds spread smooth in flash floods. Not a sandpiper, plover, bunting, or pipit did we see in the whole area. We began to think that there was not a bird of any sort there when in from the right swung an arctic skua crying *error, error,* in precisely the shrill tone of voice I had heard so many times on Southampton Island in the summer of 1930.

For Finnur the fact that the skua had come toward the jeep meant only one thing: we were close to a nest. Out the three of us got. Presently someone sighted a light brown

At Last—The Golden Plover Chick / 203

spot—something that didn't look hard or dark enough for a rock. The "something" was two well-developed young arctic skuas, crouching side by side, heads down. They were not nearly old enough to fly, but their wing and tail quills were fairly long. Their upper parts were still fairly well covered with shaggy down, which moved back and forth in the wind. The old birds flew about us gracefully, voicing their protest.

Driving farther, we found ourselves in the midst of a veritable colony of arctic skuas, all of them dark. This colonial breeding of the species was, we were informed, largely restricted to the outwash plains of southeastern Iceland, but concentrations had also been observed in northeastern Iceland and at the heads of fjords indenting the north coast.

In what was obviously primarily an arctic skua habitat we were surprised to come upon scattered pairs of great skuas, and one of these large birds entertained us with an unexpected display of injury-feigning. Knowing how fearsome a great skua could be when swooping from the sky, we looked on with amazement as one of the big birds toppled over onto its side, emitted peevish cries, and waved one wing weakly. What a way for a great skua to behave!

For me the most interesting fact of all about this stretch of dark-gray desert was that both the arctic skua and great skua were nesting in it. Finnur assured us that the great skuas never killed and ate the adult arctic skuas as they did the fulmars. As for the eggs and chicks, he was not so sure. Each species was a confirmed pirate, there was no gainsaying that; each might on occasion devour the chicks or eggs of the other species if the nests were left unguarded.

I was much impressed by the fact that we continued to

see dark arctic skuas. Not a single individual with white underparts had we thus far seen in the south of Iceland. Finnur informed us that most of the arctic skuas of Iceland were dark, but that 10 per cent in the southeastern part, 20 per cent in the southwestern part, and 30 per cent in the northern part of the island were light-phased. Nowhere in the American Arctic had I seen many all-dark birds. The distribution of the two phases in Iceland called to mind the puzzling distribution of the dichromatism in our North American screech owl, the several southern and eastern races of which came in both red and gray phases, the several western subspecies—from Canada to Mexico—which came in the gray phase only.

We drove northward a short distance from the main highway to photograph a lovely waterfall, Skógafoss (pronounced *Skó-wa-foss*), which plunged without break from the edge of the high interior to the level of the plain. It was possible to walk right into the spray at the foot of the fall; indeed, having once found this stuff of which rainbows are made, we had a hard time getting away from it. Sewall adored the rainbows. He climbed about in all directions looking at and photographing them, never seeming to get enough of them. But when the wind blew rainbow-bedizened spray over us as we were eating luncheon, I took note that with each of the three moves we made to what we hoped would be a drier spot, Sewall moved with us.

The roar, the tumult, the terrific power of the cataract held me spellbound; but what impressed me even more was the tininess of the fulmars that flew to and from their nesting places far, far above us. Some of these nesting spots

At Last—The Golden Plover Chick / 205

must have been soaking wet all summer long, for they were very close to the water.

Below the fall the stream wandered about, its banks nowhere very steep. In the vicinity of a broad sandbar several oystercatchers were feeding. When I approached the birds, most of them flew off, but the two that remained set up such an outcry that I felt sure I was near a nest or chicks. The chick that I finally found and ran down could not fly at all and part of its plumage was still downy, but it was nearly as heavy as an adult. Finnur said that this was a very late date for so young a bird.

Shortly after we left Skógafoss we ran into a rainstorm. The sky grew suddenly dark, a wind whipped up, and we were obliged to slow down. The rain ended suddenly, even as it had started, and lo, we were in the dust once more!

With only a word from Finnur as to what he intended to do, we turned south on the west side of a fair-sized river, following a rough, winding road to the river's mouth. Here, for the second time since coming to Iceland, I saw a well-defined breeding colony of great black-backed gulls. The species was widely distributed in Iceland, but it was especially common along the south coast, notably on the fluvioglacial plains known as *sandar*. Here the great skua and arctic skua also lived in considerable numbers, the three species forming a sort of *triumtyrannate* based on the respect all thieves are obliged to have for other thieves, the marvel of the arrangement being that any one species found enough to eat. The absence of such species as terns or shorebirds from these *sandar* was noticeable. Presumably the great black-back and the two species of skua lived on offal and on other forms of animal life than birds.

SKÚMUR

Great skua chick caught on the outwashed fluvial plains
near Vík, southern Iceland,
and painted direct from life July 22, 1958.

HEIDLÓA

Newly hatched golden plover chick captured near
the road from Reykjavík to Thingvellir
and painted direct from life July 29, 1958.

Before reaching Reykjavík, we stopped long enough to obtain two ringed plovers and two golden plovers, the latter handsome adult males in early stages of the postnuptial molt. We watched the golden plovers a long while before shooting them, for I clung to a wisp of hope that I would somewhere find a small chick. By this time I was almost resigned to the fact that for all our searching we had not yet seen a newly hatched chick of this really abundant species.

That evening at dinner we had occasion to remember a broad river we had crossed during the day, the Thjorsá, Iceland's largest stream. Our hosts were Dr. Günter Timmermann and his wife, delightful Germans who spent part of each year in Reykjavík, who lived in an apartment in our big apartment house on Birkimelur, and who had rented one of their rooms to the Pettingills for the summer. The principal item of the meal was a glorious big trout Dr. Timmermann himself had caught in the Thjorsá. Dr. Timmermann's chief interest was those curious feather-eating insects, the Mallophaga; but he was well informed about Iceland birds. He presented Sewall and me each with a copy of his opus on Iceland birds. This definitive work, published in German, was titled *Die Vögel Islands.*

On July 24 there was great excitement in camp, for Ed Dana and his wife, Doris, lifelong friends of the Pettingills from Maine, arrived. They were to stay in Iceland a few days then go on to the British Isles, taking the Pettingills with them. Sewall and Eleanor met them at the airport and saw them properly settled in the Hotel Borg, while I, hardly knowing which way to turn, continued to ply my trade.

A big cardboard box had come from the Vestmannaeyjar, in it two shearwaters and two storm petrels for me. Fortunately the box had been put promptly into a freezer, so that there was no need to worry about those valuable specimens. What did worry me was the great skua, which needed very much to be skinned; the melanistic arctic skua that I wanted to sketch before skinning; and the four plover specimens. Since the ringed plovers were small and in danger of going to pieces, I skinned them out first. Then I tackled a painting of a golden plover, working out intricate details of color pattern with an unskinned specimen before me. My drawing showed the bird standing on a piece of lava rock that I had picked up near the Thjorsá. I managed to finish the painting and to skin out both golden plovers before dinner. There was no time for the skuas.

The day wound up with an informal showing of all my drawings and with late dinner together—the Gudmundssons, Danas, Pettingills, and I all at one big table. During that festive, somewhat formal meal I found it great fun glancing now and then at Eleanor, always beautiful, always stylish, remembering how she looked swinging on that rope between Hellisey and the *Lundi*; at Sewall, always *distingué*, remembering him on that dizzy pinnacle, a red-shirted avenging angel standing on a needle, as it were, photographing baby gannets; and at Finnur, powerful, serious, intelligent of face, remembering him as he scampered up that steep slope east of Vík. As for Finnur's wife, Doris, and Ed, I had never been afield with them so their happy faces conjured up no cliff, no canyon, no tide rip. What a dinner it was!

To remember indeed! The following day might, but for the forbearance of my landlady, have been my last in that elegant room on Birkimelur. The arctic skua gave me no trouble; after drawing it, I skinned it out. But the great skua, having lain about for some days without refrigeration at any time, smelled bad, and when I started skinning it, the odor was too much for Sigrídur Einarsdóttir. The sound of windows being swiftly opened should have warned me. I caught a glimpse of the handsome lady moving about as if wondering how to escape. "Couldn't you do your work somewhere else, Professor? Maybe in the bathroom?" she queried.

The fact is that as one works with a slowly decomposing specimen one becomes accustomed to the odor. I was wholly unaware of the discomfort the smell was causing. Genuinely sorry, I moved everything as rapidly as I could down to "Big Blue," which was parked in front of the apartment building. But the smell was not the only cause for complaint. Several of my specimens had had Mallophaga on them and these thin, tiny lice had crawled from the plumage and cotton wrappings onto the clean wood of certain drawer bottoms. Sigrídur had been much distressed by the presence of these external parasites. Some of them had, she averred, been biting her. I felt sure that Mallophaga never bit human beings, but the thought crossed my mind that such specimens as the fulmar might have had fleas on them and that fleas did bite people. Alas, the damage had been done. I had brought live birds into the beautiful room time after time. I had tried to keep things clean, but what a mess I had caused when I had fallen into the ditch! I had tried to come and go quietly, but my models had done a lot of cheeping, squeaking, and scratching, that I knew full well.

"I would ask you to leave, Professor, but you are supposed to be an important man and your work must be important. I said you could stay here. You can, Professor. We are friends, yes?"

At Last—The Golden Plover Chick / 209

As Sigrídur reads this, she will recall that statements were made about the need for scrubbing, for fumigation, and the like. The important fact is that the squall passed, the Professor did his bird skinning in the truck from that hour on, and the work continued. Indeed, before many days had passed, Sigrídur had a cross-country trip in "Big Blue," with the Professor himself at the wheel—but I am getting ahead of my story.

For me the last week or so of July was a scramble of drawing, skinning, and feverish dashes in search of specimens. The Danas and Pettingills were to depart on the twenty-eighth. Before that date they traveled together to places the Pettingills knew about. I went with them on a picnic to "Harlequin River"—the swift stream to which we had given that name because the Pettingills had seen harlequins there in May. This was a species I still felt I did not know very well, and I was more than eager to obtain a chick. The river was the outlet of Medalfellsvatn. Along the river we saw eight harlequins—all of them adult females or young birds, or possibly adult males in eclipse plumage. During one of our evenings together, Finnur took us all to the studio of a famous photographer, Magnús Jóhannsson. There we had the pleasure of seeing a remarkable film, taken in northwest Iceland, showing the home life of white-tailed eagles and gyrfalcons. Eagles and gyrfalcons were rare birds. I remember especially the bigness of the beak of the white-tailed eagle, the bird the Icelanders called the *örn* or *haförn*.

I expected to feel a bit lost without the Pettingills, but there was no time for loneliness. On July 29 I dug right in on the shearwater and storm petrel specimens, all of which came out well. Too, I started a gyrfalcon drawing, this time using as a model a fine museum specimen lent me by Finnur. This drawing later was used by the Icelandic government in making a new twenty-five-*krónur* postage stamp.

On the evening of July 29 Árni Waag brought to my room a young bird painter named Arnthór Gardarsson. The three of us had a good time looking at my sketches and discussing Arnthór's pen-and-ink drawings, some of which I had seen. The evening went rapidly. About nine o'clock I happened to mention that one of the keenest disappointments of the summer was my failure to obtain a newly hatched golden plover chick.

The effect of the statement was instantaneous. A special, almost a predatory look came into Arnthór's face. "I saw a golden plover's nest only a day or so ago—over near the road to Thingvellir. The eggs were pipped. They would be hatching about now," he said.

"Do you think you could find the nest again?" I asked. The question was not an idle one, for unless nests of this sort are marked in some way, they may be very hard to rediscover.

"I know where it is," was Arnthór's succinct reply.

It took me about five minutes to change to field garb, and we were on our way. Both Árni and Arnthór were nicely dressed, and I wondered what I might be getting them in for, but neither said a word about changing clothes. By this time I knew the routes out of the city fairly well. It was not long before we reached the Thingvellir turnoff and began climbing.

My companions had occasion to discuss which of the side-roads would get us to the nest most expeditiously. The light was fading. Furthermore, it was beginning to rain, gently but convincingly. How wonderful it was to drive along an unpaved road without raising a dust! At my friends' suggestion we turned left. After we had followed a narrow road for some distance, Arnthór decided that we would be better off on the next side road farther east. The road we were on was graded and there seemed to be no easy way to turn around, so I started backing.

My friends agree that I am better as a bird artist than as a driver. Before long my neck tired of watching the road back of us, I made the mistake of thinking that I could drive by dead reckoning, and off we went—not far enough to turn over or to land in a ditch, but with one wheel well down over the narrow shoulder and the differential deep in gravel. The agile Árni, fearing that we might roll over, had opened the door on his side and hopped out. At first I feared he was hurt, but I soon saw that he was all right. This was a new experience for me. I thought for a time that the extra gears would pull us out, but they didn't. The rain continued.

Árni suggested that Arnthór and I climb to the plover's nest while he, Árni, would go for help. The area was wholly new to me and I must say I had grave doubts that we would ever see that nest. But Arnthór seemed to know exactly what he was doing. We walked for quite a distance northeastward, lost sight of the truck entirely, and presently heard, not far in front of us, the gentle cries of golden plovers! I continue to consider it remarkable that Arnthór, having reached a certain undistinguished hillock in this darkly veiled wilderness, looked about him, took a step in one direction, two steps in another, and walked straight to that nest in which were four of the most beautiful creatures I had ever laid eyes on. The whole thing just didn't seem possible. Mention, a little more than an hour before, of need for a plover chick; a drive; an accident; an uphill walk through the rain; and this! I could see immediately that the chicks were like those of the American golden plover in having a bright, spangled appearance. We took two specimens and left the nest so that the parent might return to brood the remaining two.

When we returned to "Big Blue," we found a goodly company of men and boys, another huge truck (on the road), and a beaming Árni. "It won't be long now," he said, motioning toward still another truck that was approaching rapidly.

While the men were attaching a heavy chain to the front of "Big Blue," I drew Árni aside and said, "Remember that I want to pay for this help. You let me know a fair price, and I'll pay it gladly." At first Árni merely demurred, as if a trifle embarrassed or at a loss to decide what such help might be worth. When I mentioned payment again, he said, this time in no uncertain tone, "Now please, *please*, just let me handle all this!"

By this time another chain or rope had been attached to "Big Blue's" side to keep it from toppling over. I sat at the wheel, the truck ahead moved forward, the chain became taut, there was an instant of hesitation, almost of indecision, and out we came without the slightest difficulty. A turning-around place was pointed out to us, there were shouts of farewell, and the helpers withdrew.

Back we went to Reykjavík. At their respective doors I delivered Árni and Arnthór and returned to Birkimelur—two golden plover chicks to the good. I made the longed-for sketch early the following morning.

On the last day of July, I had "Big Blue" lubricated, saw to it that one of the tires was repaired, and rejoiced over a package of white corn meal sent by my friend Bob Furman in Oklahoma City. Little could Bob have realized how much that pound of corn meal would mean to me! Corn meal was one of the items I could not seem to find in Iceland.

Arnthór Gardarsson sent me a young black-headed gull specimen he had found dead on July 21. I asked Árni Waag to help me write a label which would tell exactly where the specimen was found. The locality reads: Ástjörn, Gardah- reppur, Gullbringusýsla, S. W. Iceland.

XXVII

Trip to Grindavík, A Mouse,

An Eventful Evening

ON FRIDAY, the first day of August, Árni Waag guided me
to Hafurbjarnarstadir, the farmstead of Hákon Vilhjálmsson, a man famed as Iceland's chief bander or "ringer" of
birds. The farmstead was southwest of Reykjavík, beyond
the air base at Keflavík. The Pettingills had been there in
mid-June to photograph a pair of nesting gray phalaropes.
They had told me wondrous things about Hákon and the
methods he used. I was very keen to talk with this man and
to see his equipment.

With us on that dry, dusty morning was the intrepid
Sigrídur Einarsdóttir, whom we were to take as far as Grindavík, a village in which her sister-in-law was living. I tried
to explain to Sigrídur that the trip in "Big Blue" might not
be entirely comfortable. I mentioned the noise, the dust,
and the probability that the road would be rough, but Sigrídur was not to be dissuaded. Dressed nicely, and with only

a small traveling bag, she appeared at exactly the moment named for departure, took one of the little side seats back of the broad front seat, and sat there as if in perfect comfort until we got to Grindavík. I seem to recall her asking once for a match—her cigarette needed lighting. We inquired if she would like to ride in the front seat, but she insisted that she was "quite comfortable" where she was.

I can think of only one English word capable of doing the Keflavík road justice—the adjective "terrible." Once upon a time it may well have been a good highway, but it had been overused season after season and it had gone steadily from bad to worse. "Big Blue" was accustomed to vagaries in roads and in drivers, but the road to Keflavík was in a special category. The side road to Grindavík, which led through kilometer after kilometer of unglaciated postglacial lava, was perfection itself by comparison.

When we arrived at Grindavík, Sigrídur invited us to stay long enough to meet her sister-in-law. This we were more than happy to do, but we had not expected to sit down at a bountifully spread table, nor to find ourselves part of a conversation concerning art exhibits, museums, abstractionists, and the *avant garde* elements in American and European culture. With real regret we tore ourselves away. There was no telling what extra work a side trip of this sort might entail. Experience with Árni had taught me that he was a *productive* companion. He had a way of finding things. And finding things meant work for me.

We took a walk along the shore before leaving the immediate vicinity, and I was surprised at the numbers of birds we found—chiefly oystercatchers and other shore birds, but also meadow pipits and a trim little merlin which appeared without warning, flew swiftly past us not far above ground, and was still flying when last we saw it. A memorable experience on that pretty stretch of meadowland was overturning a bit of driftwood and discovering a mouse. This was the first small mammal of any sort that I had seen in Iceland. It looked very much like an American deer mouse or white-footed mouse of the genus *Peromyscus*, but actually it belonged to a wholly different genus—*Apodemus*. It was what Englishmen, as well as the poet Robert Burns, called a field mouse, a long-tailed species not indigenous to Iceland but carried there in cargoes from the Continent. I cornered it, had a good look at it, but decided not to try to capture it for I had not brought my skinning kit with me. The species is found throughout Iceland, being abundant in many areas.

Not far from Keflavík we found a fairly large breeding colony of arctic terns. I was hoping to obtain a specimen in the prettily marbled first flight plumage, but the only chicks we could find were still downy. Many of the season's young birds probably were flying strongly by this time, but we did not see any of them.

In a wholly different area, well back from the sea, we came upon a considerable flock of full-grown, nonbreeding terns, all of them in what appeared at first glance to be winter plumage. The specimens we collected from this flock had white foreheads, were white below, and had black bills and feet. They were in the so-called *"portlandica"* plumage, the first summer plumage, in which the species was not known to breed. Our friend Finnur had reported seeing "tight flocks" of these nonbreeding *"portlandica"* birds resting together on the outskirts of large terneries. These flocks, when put to flight, had mingled with the breeding birds in the air,

Trip to Grindavík, ... | 217

but when all of them had settled, the nonbreeding birds had formed a flock by themselves apart from the colony.

At Hákon's birdbanding station we saw some ingenious bird-catching apparatus—big, low, triangular, woven-wire traps set for shore birds in the sand and traps of other sorts with entrances designed to guide the birds gently in, but never out. The traps were covered with fish netting, not wire, so the birds would not injure themselves when they flew up, trying to escape. Especially remarkable was a long line of planks extending across a wide stubble field—planks set thickly with little snares for catching golden plovers by the feet. Hákon explained that the summer had so far been "dead" for him. In 1957 he had caught and banded over two thousand birds, but this year he had caught only a few. In good years the species he caught in greatest numbers were turnstones, knots, purple sandpipers, and dunlins.

As we watched a scattered company of dunlins feeding near one of the big traps, an arctic skua flew past. It was, as usual, dark all over, almost black. We could see that it was carrying a fluttering small bird in its beak. It alighted near the water's edge, shook, battered, and nibbled at its prey until the fluttering ceased, and swallowed the little bird whole. Never did it stand on or tear at its prey, as a falconiform bird surely would have. We decided that the little bird probably was a meadow pipit.

On our way back to Reykjavík I became acquainted with a bird I had never had much of a chance to observe—the lesser black-backed gull. A small colony of these gulls were nesting in flat but well-drained, rather rocky ground two kilometers or so in from the sea. We did not find any young birds, but we found an empty nest in a low-lying place among some rocks and Árni shot one of the adults for me. I was interested in noting that the tarsi and toes of the specimen were quite yellow.

The lesser black-back was, I recalled, one of the several bird species known to have established itself in Iceland since the turn of the century. This advent of a bird from the Eurasian continent, or from the British Isles, was believed to be the result of two factors—"biological success" in its established range and amelioration of climate great enough to make habitable in summer such subarctic land areas as Iceland. Dr. Gudmundsson's published statements had made clear that the lesser black-back had first been taken in Iceland in 1913, that it had begun to breed about 1928, that it was now well established at many localities along and near the south coast, but that it had continued to be strictly migratory.

On August 3, Árni and I made another try for harlequins at Medalfellsvatn. We followed two fairly large streams well back into the hills, but found no harlequins anywhere. In the river below the lake we came upon a hen red-breasted merganser with a large brood, one of which Árni caught with a strong, short-handled hand net. On August 4, Árni and I went to the lake country southeast of Reykjavík hoping to obtain a scaup chick. The day was raw and foul, with altogether too much wind and dust for comfort. I had a high old time chasing a hen scaup and her brood under a bridge near which Árni, skillfully hidden, was lying in wait. He came very close to catching one of the ducklings, too.

An evening Árni, his wife, and I had together turned out to be an eventful one. I had asked my friends to dine with me at one of Reykjavík's bright spots, a fine restaurant called

Trip to Grindavík, . . . / 219

Naust. This word meant something like "harbor" or "home port." We had eaten one or two courses when it became apparent that a special function of some sort was beginning. At a hollow rectangle of tables in the middle of the room, about thirty men and women, most of them young, were seating themselves. They were well, even elegantly, dressed. A priest or clergyman was with them. Curiosity got the better of us, of course, and our waiter told us that all these people were Hungarian refugees, that four of the couples had been married that very day, and that this was part of the wedding celebration.

The newly married couples looked happy, but there was nothing hilarious, nothing ebullient about the behavior of any of the party. Between courses, just before the dessert, I believe, the clergyman rose in a dignified way, spoke in a gentle, affectionate tone of voice, and said what were obviously moving words. Tears began to flow. We, the spectators, hardly knew how to feel and certainly did not know what to do.

Suddenly, as if afraid that dolor might get the upper hand of the evening, one of the Hungarians stood up, proposed that a song be sung, and the singing started. Not a single tune of the many that were sung did I recognize, for they were all Hungarian. Tears continued, but there was laughter too, some of it very blithesome. When the Hungarian national anthem was sung, we all stood up.

It was becoming quite an evening. When the singing of the Hungarian group subsided, I heard the scraping of a chair, the clearing of a healthy throat, and the booming voice of an Englishman saying some very friendly things to and about the Hungarians. There was hearty applause. The gentleman's name was Maynard. He had a party of five or six persons with him.

It is hard to explain what I now did. The singing of the Hungarians had stirred me. Mr. Maynard's kindly words had stirred me. I gave Árni fair warning that I was about to do something and up I stood, speaking for the United States of America—a country I was very proud of at the moment—saying that when I got back to the University of Oklahoma I would look up all the Hungarian students I could find and tell them of this wonderful evening we had all had together. My little speech was followed by hearty applause.

The next person to rise was a German, I believe. Then someone spoke for France, and someone for Switzerland. All this was, of course, wholly impromptu, wholly unrehearsed, and therefore extremely impressive.

The next move seemed to astonish everyone, though it may have been planned. The restaurant's manager came forward, said some friendly words in Icelandic, and informed us that champagne "on the house" was about to be served.

A young Icelander from Mr. Maynard's table slipped across the room, sat down by me, and said, "It was wonderful hearing you speak for the United States. I have been there. I want to go again." Before I knew it, hands were beckoning us across the room and the Maynard party and mine joined forces. In the Maynard party was one of Iceland's most distinguished artists, an abstractionist named Nína Tryggvadóttir, some of whose works were hanging in the National Gallery.

I was carried away by all this—carried back, too, to the meetings of the old Savage Club at Cornell, where we used to drink beer and entertain each other with songs, stories, tap dances, and sleight of hand. One of my favorite songs at the Savage Club had been "Bohemia Hall." "Why not sing it now?" I kept asking myself. "Go ahead! Sing it for them!" I walked up to the pianist on the far corner of the stage, asked him if he knew "Bohemia Hall," thought I saw him nod his head, and heard myself announcing that I would sing.

I suspect that Árni would gladly have disappeared through the floor. But he listened politely along with everyone else and joined in the applause. The ice, if ever there had been such a thing as ice in Iceland, was pretty well thawed by this time.

Árni's words, when we parted that night, reflected my own thoughts precisely, "Never, *never* in this world did I expect to spend an evening like this one!"

XXVIII

End of Summer

Now THAT I HAD a direct-from-life drawing of a newly hatched golden plover chick, I felt that the summer had a right to be called successful. True, I had not seen a white-tailed eagle, nor found a black-tailed godwit's nest, nor obtained a scaup chick; but when I contemplated the remarkable experiences I had had, the wonderful people I had come to know, the fine specimens I had obtained, and the thirty-some drawings I had made, I felt that in some ways this was the most productive summer I had ever lived. Perhaps I was learning, at long last, how to make the precious hours count!

It was good during those early days of August to become a bit better acquainted with Reykjavík. I visited the National Art Gallery, making a point of finding Nína Tryggvadóttir's bold abstractions. I wandered about the bookstores—some of them the most interesting I had ever been in. I idled, actually idled, along the waterfront, sauntering to the end of the principal pier, spelling out letter by letter the strange names of the vessels, identifying as best I could the oddly plumaged gulls that I continued to see. Some of these puzzling gulls were, I finally decided, herring gulls; others were lesser black-backs. Never did I walk along Tjarnargata without gazing in wonder at the hundreds of mallards. There were no little chicks any more, now that summer was ending, but a few hens were still accompanied by good-sized ducklings, some of which darted about snatching up flies just as the newly hatched broods had been wont to do a few weeks before. If I looked for molted feathers, I could find them, but nowhere was the lake shore unsightly because of them. So many times had I seen people picking away withered flowers in the old cemetery and along the walks in Austurvöllur that I wondered whether some corps of feathergatherers might be responsible for the cleanliness of the water's edge, but certainly I never saw anyone picking up feathers.

I wondered how long the drakes in eclipse plumage would continue to be neat and whether any of them had already passed through the flightless stage of the molt. If the reproductive cycle of these Iceland mallards proceeded as did that of our American mallards, every adult drake on Tjörnin would have a shiny-green head, a snow-white collar, and a mahogany-colored chest by the end of November at the very latest. What a dropping out of feathers there presently would be! And virtually every one of the molted body feathers would have a pattern suggestive of the hen bird. The thought crossed my mind that in wild country mallards would about this time be seeking sequestered spots in which to pass the difficult flightless period; but here the birds had so long known complete safety that they made no attempt to secrete themselves. A thought of another sort I could not crowd from my mind: what a marvelous place was Tjörnin for a study of mallard behavior! A Konrad Lorenz would by this time have found himself a grassy spot and campstool and be on speaking terms with the whole mallard population! It is a comment on some contrary streak in my nature that I never once threw a piece of bread or handful of grain to those mallards. I greatly enjoyed them, but was perfectly happy watching them at a distance, feeling no desire to have them follow me about.

I planned to fly back to New York on August 15. Finnur Gudmundsson had provided me with two large, well-made wooden boxes for mailing my bird skins to America. I moved the well-dried specimens from my room to the museum. Gladly would I have settled down to a week or so of unhurried packing, of walks across the meadowlands between the busy Hringbraut and the airfield, of visits to certain streets whose house fronts and gardens never failed to delight me. But the gods, ably assisted by Finnur, decreed otherwise. My last few days in Iceland were as busy as the first had been.

At six o'clock Friday evening, August 8, Finnur called for me. This time I was to be part of the family, and we were all going to a lake known as Laugarvatn (pronounced *Lói-gar-vah-tun*). Into this fine body of water ran swift streams along which Finnur had seen harlequin ducks. My friend had not forgotten my special interest in harlequins. He was interested in them himself, for there were no harlequin chicks in his extensive museum collections.

How all of us and our luggage got into that one jeep I do

not know, but in we climbed—Gudrídur Gísladóttir (Finnur's slender, delicately beautiful wife), his two delightful
daughters, Helga and Gudrún Finnsdóttir (who, on the occasion of our first meeting had told me that their favorite
American movie star was "perhaps" Tony Curtis), the big,
powerful Finnur, and I, and off we went. For a wonder the
sky was overcast and fine rain was falling. There was no dust.
The countryside was beautifully green and fresh looking.
We stopped for a picnic supper on high land near the Sog,
the river flowing southward out of Thingvallavatn. As we
ate, we witnessed the bringing to gaff of a big salmon. We
could observe every movement of the fisherman and of his
weary prize, for we had good binoculars. The salmon, which
flashed silver as the light struck it, must have weighed all
of six pounds. As we sped along the slope above Laugarvatn
and another big lake called Apavatn, we crossed several "harlequin streams." Some of these we would visit on the morrow.

Our headquarters for the weekend, a school which served
in summer as a hostelry, we reached about dark. Off to the
northeast, at slightly lower elevation, lay Laugarvatn. The
light rain continued.

Early the following morning Finnur and I drove back to
one of the little "harlequin streams," parked the jeep, and
set to work. Each of us carried a package of lunch. Finnur
had a shotgun. We decided first to walk downstream from
the bridge through country that reminded me of the richest
grassy tundra I had seen in the American Arctic. Not many
flowers were still in bloom, and I looked in vain for a bumble-
bee. When I asked Finnur where the bees were, he replied
that he was not sure he had seen a single bee that whole summer. The extreme dryness of the season may have been re-

sponsible for this. After we had walked a mile or so, we entered godwit habitat and Finnur shot a young bird which was well grown, able to fly perfectly, but much shorter-billed than an adult. It was in beautiful juvenal plumage. I was much impressed by the fact that its bill was not even slightly recurved.

We followed the meanderings of the stream for about an hour and found no harlequin. Having made our way back to the bridge as directly as possible, we walked upstream. Here, where the slope was steep, there were rapids, cataracts, and shallow gorges. We failed to find a harlequin, but from low willows hiding a stretch of shore we routed four teal, all stub-winged and unable to fly, which shot off downstream in a close-knit group, heading straight for a long stretch of white water. I had always thought of teal as birds of ponds and quiet pools. Certainly they were not divers in the usual sense of the word. Yet into the rapids they plunged, hidden from sight completely for a time, then out in the froth and spray, bobbing along like so many corks. Having made their getaway, they hugged the farther bank. At the foot of the rapids they disappeared into the vegetation.

A mile above the bridge the stream forked. On we climbed, into high country, following the east branch, allowing no pool or stretch of bank to escape inspection. Reaching a sort of escarpment, we crossed over to the other branch and returned to the junction. By this time, needless to say, we both had given up all hope of keeping our feet dry. I was surprised by our failure to see or hear either golden plovers or whimbrels. A notable color element of the landscape was the bright green of the long scarves of algae in the clear water.

Having climbed to the top of a knob, we crossed to a new valley, pausing now and then to pick blueberries or to survey the stream with our binoculars. Nowhere were the blueberries abundant and only a few of them were ripe. I continued to be amazed by the scarcity of birds. Only occasionally did we see even a meadow pipit. One redpoll flew over.

As we moved downslope the stream bed flattened out a bit, but the water continued to be swift and noisy. Suddenly we found ourselves at the upper end of a narrow, not very large but deep impoundment, beyond which the main house of a prosperous-looking farmstead was partly visible. The stream entered the impoundment as a steep, shallow riffle. A high dam at the opposite end was equipped with a generator which furnished the farmstead with electricity. At first we did not see the harlequins, for they kept low in a shadowed part of the pool, but when we looked upstream from the dam the four birds were plainly visible. Four harlequins, a mother and three chicks! The chicks were far larger than the "downies" I needed, but any sort of harlequin was wildly exciting. I was surprised that they stayed on the surface. The old bird went under now and then, but the chicks did not seem to want to dive.

For a busy half-hour Finnur and I clung to the belief that by some trick of our trade we could catch one of those chicks alive. We chased them, threw rocks at them, forced them into the narrow upper end of the pool, eventually, to our great satisfaction, saw two of them scrambling up the riffle. But so clever were these two at hiding that we did not even see them again until, after another half-hour of waiting in a spot out of sight of the ducks, we perceived that the mother and brood were together again, swimming confidently in the middle of the impoundment.

It was obvious that if we were to obtain a chick we would have to use the gun. Finnur, explaining that permission to shoot should be obtained from the owner of the farmstead, suggested that we think about the matter a while as we ate lunch. This I was more than glad to do. I know of no human activity more certain to work up an appetite than chasing harlequins in Iceland.

Finnur's trip to the house required a full half-hour. On his return he informed me that it would be agreeable to all concerned for us to shoot one of the chicks. The hen and her brood were known to every member of the family. The nest had been on a steep bank below the dam. The brooding mother had been watched day after day. I must confess that going after that agreed-upon chick seemed a little like hunting down a household pet, but the deed had to be done were I ever to know what a young harlequin looked like. We shot the chick without trouble, picking it from the water just as it entered the sluice.

We examined the specimen carefully. On its head and neck were tattered patches of down, remains of the natal plumage, but there was no way of telling from the plumage pattern in general what that of the newly-hatched chick had been. The specimen would be interesting and valuable in any collection, and assuredly I would make a drawing of it, but it was not what I needed.

"I neglected to mention," said Finnur somewhat formally, "a stipulation. We were to obtain the harlequin chick, then I was to bring you to the house for coffee. So now we will go."

We walked to the house, a fine large structure, noble in its simplicity. The farm's name was Eyvindartunga. Trees that looked to me like two species of mountain ash grew near the front door. We were cordially received by the farmer himself, a fine-looking young man named Jón Teitsson, who led us to an end room whose windows looked out upon the green valley and the shining Laugarvatn. In the middle of the room was a small table gleaming with damask linen and the finest of handmade silver. Two chairs were at the table, one for Finnur, one for me, and there we sat while Jón's sweet-faced mother stood, beaming upon us and making clear with graceful gestures that we were to help ourselves to the bread spread with butter if we pleased, or to the little doughnuts, or to the raisin cake, or to the bread spread with cheese. There must have been at least ten kinds of delicacies before us, not to mention the coffee, which Jón insisted on pouring whenever a cup showed the slightest sign of being anything but full. Not a word of English did these wonderful people speak, but Finnur told them of my work and I found it easy to say exactly what I wanted to say, knowing that Finnur would give them the meaning of my words. How sorry I was that I had none of my drawings with me!

Here was a family I would like to know better, a farmstead I hated to leave. For the first time since coming to Iceland I was thoroughly annoyed with myself for my inability to speak Icelandic. I had been somewhat sorry several times, but this time the feeling went deep.

Finnur and I walked to the jeep and drove back to the hostelry. Dinner was served exactly at seven o'clock, so my painting work was interrupted. The more I looked at the young godwit, the lovelier its color seemed. Its head, neck, and breast were a rich fawn color.

I have no recollection of going to sleep that night or of awakening refreshed. What I remember is that our hunt for harlequins continued with the rising of the sun and with a clambering upward toward the headwaters of another river. This time we were in stunningly beautiful country, the most soul-stirring spot of all for me being a dark chasm at the upper end of which a snow-white cataract was partly visible under and between dark, overhanging walls. The glassy smoothness of the stream moving down the chasm awed me; I watched it entranced, unable to take my eyes away. The vegetation was utterly lovely—ferns that had never lacked for moisture all season long, luxuriant birch trees, deep green moss, dripping wet.

No harlequin, no harlequin, nowhere a harlequin! We decided to try the lower part of the river, the long stretch that wandered through the flat grassland out to the big lake. Soon we began seeing birds once more—whimbrels, ringed plovers, and godwits, the last where the grass was luxuriant.

When we were within about a mile of the river's mouth, we came upon some harlequins—this time a company of two hens and several smallish chicks, hugging the very edge of the water under a not very high, but overhanging bank. Adults and young alike had perfected the technique of scooting along against the swift current, coming to rest occasionally on little muddy projections. The swiftness of the water did not seem to disturb them in the slightest; indeed, they seemed to like the very swift places best of all, and I was astonished at how quickly the whole company were able to vanish through the simple procedure of slipping under the surface, drifting downstream, and coming up beneath a bit of shaggy, curled-over turf.

Once more Finnur and I thought surely we could catch a chick alive either by forcing it out of the water, by snatching it from a riffle, or by creeping up on its hiding place. We worked on opposite sides of the stream. I kept my eye on the ducks and motioned to Finnur exactly where the birds were. He sneaked up on them on all fours, ready to reach his long arm down or to plunge in after them if necessary. Once, convinced that a chick, cut off from the rest, had taken refuge under a bit of bank below me, I leaned down, reached beneath the turf, and actually felt a kick from a soft little foot, but the bird was too quick for me and I never even saw it as it made its getaway. By this time we were barefoot and more or less wet all over, our gear was scattered thither and yon, and the look on our faces was that of fanatics.

Alas, we had finally to use the gun. To my great delight we found that the chicks were still in natal down. They were six or seven inches long, with necks stretched out, but the plumage pattern was obviously very much like that of the newly hatched bird.

We followed the river to its very mouth. Finnur called my attention to the lake's outlet, which seemed to be only a stone's throw from the inlet, a foible of geography I could neither explain nor recall having seen anywhere else in the world.

Before we left the low-lying grassland close to the lake, Finnur helped me obtain an adult black-tailed godwit, the first I had ever shot. The bird had been eating blueberries and crowberries. It was molting, some of the feathers of its upper parts being of the clear ashy-gray winter plumage.

Before dark I made a drawing of the harlequin chick and

of the adult godwit's head, neck, and shoulders. When I showed my work to Finnur, he called attention immediately to an error: I had shown too much recurvature in the godwit's long bill. The black-tailed godwit is comparatively straight-billed even as an adult; had I been drawing a bar-tailed godwit, a species found widely in the Old World as well as in Alaska, this noticeable recurvature of bill would have been acceptable. I was grateful for this well-timed criticism. The three-ply watercolor paper was tough. I scrubbed the drawing of the bill away with strong, stiff brushes and a sponge, let the paper dry thoroughly, erased every trace of what I had put down, and drew again. The new bill was a great improvement.

Our return to Reykjavík was all too swift. As we sped along, I realized that these might be my last close-at-hand glimpses of wild Iceland. We stopped long enough for a short climb and a look down into an extinct crater. What a land of surprises this Iceland was—a neat, friendly road running along the base of an innocent-looking rise, and just beyond this rise a yawning hole fearsome enough to make the blood run cold!

Those last days were pleasant ones. Árni Waag had an adult redshank which he had kept in the freezer for me. He wanted to watch me prepare the skin. As I worked, we discussed the study Árni had been making of redwings. He had been banding young birds, brood after brood of them, and already he had accumulated a considerable amount of data pertaining to two-broodedness; but he had had trouble catching the adults. I told him I would send him a mist net.

With this lightweight bit of apparatus hung in a shadowy place near the nests he would be able to catch the parent birds without much trouble.

I set aside part of one day for a last look at the Tjörnin mallards; for a leisurely walk about Austurvöllur, still bright with flowers; for a brief visit to my coffee place on Laekjargata and for a glimpse of the well-paved Adalstraeti, the street that once had been a track up from the sea. All these had become part of my life. I had learned to love them well.

Finnur Gudmundsson and Árni Waag, faithful friends, were at the airport to see me off. As the plane squared away for its flight across the Atlantic, I found myself wondering which of the summer's experiences would prove to be the most memorable. Would it be the capture of the Barrow's goldeneye hen on her nest at Mývatn? The climb to the top of Hellisey? The drive through the gray waste of sand east of Vík? Or might the longest-lived memories of all be not of separate experiences but rather of hour after hour, day after day, of flawless companionship; of the unexpected tenderness a man may reveal as he replaces chunks of turf; of the changes that may take place in one's mind as the true stature of a people whose language differs from one's own becomes apparent?

List of Birds Mentioned in the Text

Species whose icelandic names are given are found in Iceland; the others have never been reported from Iceland or are not found there regularly.

Common Name	Scientific Name	Icelandic Name
American Golden Plover	*Pluvialis dominica*	
American Robin (see Robin)		
Arctic Skua	*Stercorarius parasiticus*	Kjói
Arctic Tern	*Sterna paradisaea*	Kría
Barrow's Goldeneye	*Bucephala islandica*	Húsönd
Bar-tailed Godwit	*Limosa lapponica*	
Black-backed Gull	*Larus marinus*	Svartbakur
Black Duck	*Anas rubripes*	
Black Guillemot	*Cepphus grylle*	Teista
Black-headed Gull	*Larus ridibundus*	Hettumáfur

Common Name	Scientific Name	Icelandic Name
Black-tailed Godwit	Limosa limosa	Jadrakan
Brambling	Fringilla montifringilla	Fjallfinka
Brünnich's Murre	Uria lomvia	Stuttnefja
Common Eider	Somateria mollissima	Aedarfugl
Common Loon	Gavia immer	Himbrini; Brúsi
Common Murre	Uria aalge	Langvía
Common Scoter	Melanitta nigra	Hrafnsönd
Common Snipe	Capella gallinago	Hrossagaukur
Dunlin	Erolia alpina	Lóuthraell
Fulmar	Fulmarus glacialis	Fýll
Gadwall	Anas strepera	Litla Gráönd
Gannet	Moris bassana	Súla; Hafsúla
Glaucous Gull	Larus hyperboreus	Stóre hvítmáfur
Golden Plover	Pluvialis apricaria	Heidlóa
Graylag Goose	Anser anser	Grágaes
Gray Phalarope	Phalaropus fulicarius	Thórshani
Great Auk	Plautus impennis	Geirfugl
Great Black-backed Gull (see Black-backed gull)		
Greater Scaup (see Scaup)		
Greater Shearwater	Puffinus gravis	
Great Northern Diver (see Common Loon)		
Great Skua	Catharacta skua	Skúmur
Green-winged teal	Anas carolinensis	
Gyrfalcon	Falco rusticolus	Fálki, Valur
Harlequin Duck	Histrionicus histrionicus	Straumönd
Heath Hen	Tympanuchus cupido cupido	
Herring Gull	Larus argentatus	Silfurmáfur
Horned Grebe (see Slavonian Grebe)		
King Eider	Somateria spectabilis	Aedarkóngur

Common Name	Scientific Name	Icelandic Name
Kittiwake	*Rissa tridactyla*	Rita; Skegla
Knot	*Calidris canutus*	Raudbrystingur
Leach's Petrel	*Oceanodroma leucorhoa*	Stóra Saesvala
Lesser Black-backed Gull	*Larus fuscus*	Litla Svartbakur
Mallard	*Anas platyrhynchos*	Stokkönd
Manx Shearwater	*Puffinus puffinus*	Skrofa
Meadow Pipit	*Anthus pratensis*	Thúfutittlingur
Merlin	*Falco columbarius*	Smyrill
Mute Swan	*Cygnus olor*	
Northern Phalarope	(see Red-necked Phalarope)	
Oldsquaw	*Clangula hyemalis*	Hávella
Oystercatcher	*Haematopus ostralegus*	Tjaldur
Parasitic Jaeger	(see Arctic Skua)	
Pintail	*Anas acuta*	Grafönd
Ptarmigan	(see Rock Ptarmigan)	
Puffin	*Fratercula arctica*	Lundi
Purple Sandpiper	*Erolia maritima*	Sendlingur
Raven	*Corvus corax*	Hrafn
Razor-billed Auk	*Alca torda*	Álka
Red-backed Sandpiper	(see Dunlin)	
Red-breasted Merganser	*Mergus serrator*	Toppönd; Litla Toppönd
Red-necked Phalarope	*Lobipes lobatus*	Odinshani
Red Phalarope	(see Gray Phalarope)	
Redshank	*Tringa totanus*	Stelkur
Red-throated Loon	*Gavia stellata*	Lómur
Redwing	*Turdus musicus*	Skógarthröstur
Red-winged Blackbird	*Agelaius phoeniceus*	
Redpoll	*Acanthis flammea*	Audnutittlingur
Ringed Plover	*Charadrius hiaticula*	Sandlóa

List of Birds / 237

Robin	*Turdus migratorius*	
Rock Ptarmigan	*Lagopus mutus*	Rjúpa
Scaup	*Aythya marila*	Duggönd
Scoter (see Common Scoter)		
Screech Owl	*Otus asio*	
Shag	*Phalacrocorax aristotelis*	Toppskarfur
Shoveller	*Spatula clypeata*	Skeidönd
Slavonian Grebe	*Podiceps auritus*	Sefönd; Flórgodi
Snipe (see Common Snipe)		
Snow Bunting	*Plectrophenax nivalis*	Snjótittlingur; Sólskríkja
Snowy Owl	*Nyctea scandiaca*	Snaeugla
Sooty Shearwater	*Puffinus griseus*	
Sprague's Pipit	*Anthus spraguei*	
Storm Petrel	*Hydrobates pelagicus*	Litla Saesvala
Teal	*Anas crecca*	Urtönd
Thick-billed Guillemot (see Brünnich's Murre)		
Tufted Duck	*Aythya fuligula*	Skúfönd
Turnstone	*Arenaria interpres*	Tildra
Water Pipit	*Anthus spinoletta*	
Water Rail	*Rallus aquaticus*	Keldusvín
Wheatear	*Saxicola oenanthe*	Steindepill
Whimbrel	*Numenius phaeopus*	Spói
White Wagtail	*Motacilla alba*	Máríatla
White-tailed Eagle	*Haliæetus albicilla*	Örn; Haförn
Whooper Swan	*Cygnus cygnus*	Álft; Svanur
Widgeon	*Mareca penelope*	Raudhöfdaönd
Willet	*Catoptrophorus semipalmatus*	
Wren	*Troglodytes troglodytes*	Músarrindill

Index